Building People...Building Dreams

How a church can change a nation

Tom Deuschle

Foreword by Dr. John W. Stanko

NOTE: Z$ refers to Zimbabwe dollars. US$ refers to U.S. dollars.

TABLE OF CONTENTS

DEDICATION

I dedicate this book to my father and mother, Tom and Evelyn Deuschle, who have been shining examples to me and to all who know them of what it means to run the race and persevere through the hard times and the near-impossible ones. You both taught me never to quit. I also dedicate this book to the single most important person in my life, my wife, Bonnie. Without you, I would not be the man I am today, nor would I have been able to do all that God has assigned me to do. Bonnie, I love you. Finally to our children, who are the hope of the future and whom I cherish with all my heart. Tommy, Jonathan, Benjamin, Daniel, and Sarah, dream big dreams. Thank you for your love, constant support, and understanding. As we have been building people and building dreams in Zimbabwe, you still remain our primary focus, our joy, and our delight.

As this book was going to press, my friend and mentor, Dr. Ed Cole, went home to be with the Lord. I want to pay special tribute to this great man and especially dedicate this book and its use to Dr. Cole's memory. May the investment he made in my life and the lives of countless other men continue to bear fruit for many years to come. Thank you, Dr. Cole, for a life well spent.

FOREWORD

My first encounter with Zimbabwe was not a pleasant one. I had stopped in Harare on a one-day business trip in 1995, and on the way to the airport for my continuing flight to London, my briefcase was stolen, along with my passport, computer, and plane tickets. What was to be a quick stopover on my way to London became an unexpected and unwelcome stay-over. Yet today I count that mishap as a great gift from God, for that extended stay enabled me to meet Tom and Bonnie Deuschle and the Hear the Word Ministries (HTWM) team.

When I read the manuscript for this book, I thought of the words in John's gospel: "The man who saw it has given testimony, and his testimony is true" (John 19:35 NIV). Since 1995, I have visited Zimbabwe and HTWM on numerous occasions to consult, advise, work with the staff, and speak in their services. As much as anyone I am familiar with their story and operation. I have seen their ministry outreaches, and I know the people who tell their own stories on the pages that follow.

The story that Tom Deuschle tells in this book is a story of faith and failure, adventure and agony, success and sorrow. It is a story of what God can do with a man and woman who put their trust in Him. This book chronicles the journey of a church that is not content to retreat behind its stained glass windows, but one that has attempted to impact the nation in which it worships.

The HTWM leaders and members have struggled at times to do what few others have done. They have made mistakes and there have been plenty of setbacks. I think of the words of the American president, Theodore Roosevelt, who said:

It is not the critic who counts: not the man who points out how the strong man stumbles or where the doer of deeds could have done better. The credit belongs to the man who is actually in the arena, whose face is marred by dust and sweat and blood, who strives valiantly, who errs and comes up short again and again, because there is no effort without error or shortcoming, but who knows the great enthusiasms, the great devotions, who spends himself for a worthy cause; who, at the best, knows, in the end, the triumph of high achievement, and who, at the worst, if he fails, at least he fails while daring greatly, so that his place shall never be with those cold and timid souls who knew neither victory nor defeat.[1]

HTWM is a true success story of the African church and provides a model for the church the world over to follow. The HTWM story should be studied by anyone who is interested in missions, church planting, or church growth. The church should and must be involved in redeeming not only mankind but also the institutions that affect everyday life, and that is exactly what Tom Deuschle and HTWM have tried to do.

I have learned a great deal from visiting HTWM and from Tom and Bonnie. I am honored to be their friend and to be part of the HTWM ministry family. I invite you to read this book and to be challenged by its content. After you have finished, ask God what you can do to change your own world. While the inspiration of *Building People...Building Dreams* is fresh in your mind and heart, find a project upon which you can focus your faith. The HTWM story is still being written and its future chapters will include your story of what you will do once you have read this book.

May the Lord reward you, Tom and Bonnie, for your labor of love. May God grant you favor and success, Hear the Word Ministries, as you enter this new chapter of ministry and service. And reader, may God use *Building People...Building Dreams* to speak to your heart about doing something great for God!

Dr. John W. Stanko
President, PurposeQuest International
www.purposequest.com

PREFACE

I have entitled this book *Building People...Building Dreams* because that is what my wife and I have endeavored to do with our life and ministry. As I reflect on all that God has accomplished in our two decades of ministry in Africa, I realize the importance of relationships. When we were younger, we did not always recognize the value of relationships or people, but the older we got the more we appreciated what they added to our lives. The definition of synergy—"the sum of the parts is greater than the whole"—applies to my life and ministry.

We are grateful to the Lord, who called us and also sustained us. One of the ways He has done this is by bringing strategic people into our lives, just at the right moment, to teach, encourage, and motivate us.

We are deeply grateful to all our friends and family who have supported us with prayers and words of encouragement when we needed them most. To all who have given financially, your seed has fallen into good soil—not only in the ministry outreaches where we have sown, but also in the soil of our lives. With your assistance, you have afforded Bonnie, our children, and me the opportunity to do the work of God in difficult situations with the knowledge that we are supported by a network of friends and churches that really care about us and the welfare of our family. We will always cherish your friendship and faithfulness.

I want to thank some of those significant people, in their order of appearance. First are my parents, Tom and Evelyn Deuschle. Although they did not know Jesus while they were raising me, they kept me aware of a God who was watching and instilled in me the habits of faithful attendance in church and never quitting until the job was complete. To my brothers and sisters—Mary, Mark, Joe, Bill,

Bob, Margaret, and Pat—who may never have fully understood my leaving the United States to live in Africa, but have always shown an outward expression of love and acceptance for the call of God on my life. To Pastor Lou Montecalvo of Redeemer Temple who exposed me to God's love and the Holy Spirit. To Bob and Micky Baird who allowed me to teach a Bible study before I was one year old in the Lord. What were you thinking? You must have seen something I did not. To Christ for the Nations and the great instructors there who also laid foundations in my life: Sister Freda Lindsay, John Garlock, Jim Hodges, Alan Beck, Charles Munroe, Pat Pride, and the late Ron Wahlrobe. I want to thank David High for encouraging me in the early years. I am deeply grateful to Wayne Myers for teaching me faith for finances and a heart for world missions, and to David, his son, for his friendship and the phone call that changed my life.

I would not have lasted one month in the ministry if it were not for the seeds of the "faith message" planted by Fred Price. I nearly wore out his 28 tapes on the basic principles of faith, which he taught at Christ for the Nations, along with additional material I purchased from his book table. Fred Price kept mentioning a "Brother Hagin" in nearly every cassette teaching, and I am so grateful to Ray McCauley for loading me up with books and tapes by Kenneth Hagin as well as a host of other "faith" teachers and preachers. Ray has had a profound impact on my life during my entire ministry; he has been an inspiration to the nation of South Africa and to many leaders in the region. Bonnie and I would not be who we are today nor have accomplished what we have without the help we received from Rhema South Africa, and Rhema Tulsa, and all of the wonderful people who came by association, including Mark and Janet Brazee, Alphonso Belin, Fred and Cookie Brothers, and all of our friends on the staff of Rhema Bible Church in Randburg, South Africa. Others who influenced us early in the ministry were Fred and Nellie Roberts, Tim and Sally Salmon, and Ron and Antoinette Dick, along with Eben Combrinck, who were all sources of encouragement in the days before I met my wife, Bonnie. Special thanks to Ron and Joanna Kussmaul who always urged me to practice the supernatural.

As our own ministry began to grow, there were many leaders from around the world who began to find their way into our lives and into the nation of Zimbabwe. Each had a profound impact on us, and in many cases became our friends, mentors, and family. At the top of the list are Don and Marlene Ostrom, who have believed in Bonnie and me since the first time we met in 1984. They took a keen interest in our ministry and Zimbabwe and introduced us to many who had a lasting impact in our lives—most notably Pastors Casey and Wendy Treat in Seattle, Washington, who befriended us and guided us in our early years of pastoring a church. The Bonnie Breakfasts held by Wendy to help pay for Bonnie's second album were a real boost to our faith. The support they gave us in the early years, both through friendship and finances, can never be minimized.

There is not space enough to thank the many leaders who contributed to our annual Action Conferences, but I am grateful to each one for the lasting seeds they sowed into the lives of so many. These conferences could never have taken place without the support of the nation and its leaders here in Zimbabwe. Thanks to so many of the pastors and leaders who have stood by us as we have endeavored to do what many said was impossible. I could not possibly mention everyone by name but you all know who you are, and so does God. (Thankfully He keeps accurate records.)

Through Bonnie's relationships at Oral Roberts

University, we have found friends and family all over the world. Oral and Evelyn will never fully understand the impact that they have had on our ministry. First of all is the deposit in their spiritual daughter Bonnie, who constantly compared our endeavors with those of her mentor, which was not always welcomed, especially at the time. Every time we would walk on the ORU campus, something inside me would say, "If Oral could do this by faith in Tulsa, Oklahoma, I can believe God for something great by faith in Zimbabwe, Africa." Richard Roberts and George Fisher have been a constant source of encouragement to Bonnie and me, both personally and in a very unusual way financially. Richard has been prophetic in his giving into our lives and ministry. Thank you for the advice not to stop any of our outreaches or missions programs when we started to build. It was a great temptation, but one that we resisted, and today are so thankful that we did. Richard, thank you for your many trips to Zimbabwe; your seed will not return to you without a great harvest.

No building of the stature of the Celebration Center can be credited to one man. I am overwhelmed by the response of our congregation, my fellow pastors and leaders, and our business community. I cannot tell you how blessed I am to be surrounded by such great men and women. The unsung heroes are those on my building committee who stood with me for five years and at times lost heart and focus but remained true to the vision. Perhaps most importantly I appreciate my pastoral team, who allowed me to be absent from the day-to-day operation of the ministry, to miss prayer meetings and all kinds of important functions so that I could oversee the building of a church facility that has taken five long years. Although I know they would all say it has been a great growing season in their lives and would never complain, I also realize what a strain it has placed upon our congregation and our leadership, and I am deeply grateful for the faith, loyalty, and commitment they have shown.

The most important ingredient that God added to my life is my wife, Bonnie. I would not exchange my life with Bonnie for anything. For 20 years of our life and ministry together, she has followed me all around Africa and all over the world. She has given birth to our five wonderful children: Thomas, Jonathan, Benjamin, Daniel, and Sarah. As the church grew and our family enlarged, she gave herself to training leaders, raising a family, and continuing to oversee the praise and worship in the church, She has developed a wonderful ministry of praise and worship that culminated in a world-class Christmas pageant that was broadcast on national television for three consecutive years. Her tireless effort won her both acclaim and criticism. Because she worked so hard and gave of herself so sacrificially, many accused her of neglecting her children. At times it may have appeared that way from the outside, but I saw first-hand how Bonnie could easily shift gears and care for even the smallest needs of our children.

Bonnie became the example of a Proverbs 31 woman, and today her children are rising up and calling her blessed, and following in her footsteps. Our oldest son, Tommy, sings, plays trumpet and guitar, and was even featured with his mother on her latest album. Jonathan plays an aggressive lead guitar, is learning the saxophone, and also did background vocals on Bonnie's album. Benjamin is committed to playing the drums as well as singing with the family. Daniel truly has his mother's gift of music and has sung with her all over the world since he was a baby and is now practicing the violin. Sarah sang before she talked, and even at a young age sings with perfect pitch; she was also featured on Bonnie's latest album with her own song.

There are only a few men who truly act as fathers in our lives. I have had the privilege of having two. Dr. Lester Sumrall took an unusual interest in my life and in Africa in his later years of life. I will be eternally grateful for the rich deposit of faith and perseverance he imparted to me. His life filled a great void in our lives here in Africa, and he is greatly missed. Dr. Edwin Louis Cole has poured out his life into many men, all around the world. I am blessed to know him as a friend and a father in the Lord. We have worked at majoring on men and teaching that Christlikeness and manhood are synonymous. Dr. Cole not only gave his life and friendship to me, but also opened up the entire Christian Men's Network to me. I have had the great privilege of meeting the finest men in the world through this outstanding ministry, and now I can call these men my friends. Paul, Joanne, and all in the extended Cole family, thank you for taking Bonnie and me and my children into your world. John and Bruce Binkley have enriched my life and have sown their lives into the men of Africa. Jim Halek, you are going to shake the world; thank you for your friendship. There are dozens of men from the Network with whom I have had the honor of sharing my life, and I am richly blessed by the associations that God has allowed. I would not be the man nor the minister that I am today without the input I have received from these men.

Bill Bennot has been a friend since we met at Reinhard Bonnke's Fire Conference in Harare. It was no accident that we became great friends the minute we met. Not only have we worked together, but we have also dreamed of touching Africa together. With your heart for church planting in Africa, I count it a privilege to now be joined together in fulfilling the larger vision.

Those who have sown their lives into Zimbabwe and our lives through ministering here, usually with minimal financial incentive, are truly heroes of the faith. Dr. John Stanko came for a one-night visit to set up an outreach for Integrity Music, and ended up staying four days and nights, returning as many as three to four times a year for the next eight years. Thank you, John, for your practical input. Thank you for introducing us to Joseph Garlington, who has become a friend and on numerous occasions has poured times of refreshing on a dry and thirsty land. Phil Pringle and our friends from Australia have blessed us with the distinctive move of God from that continent and, along with Larry Stockstill, with a vision for cells and growth. Chris and Christine Staley and Steve and Karina Maile from the United Kingdom have been faithful friends we appreciate your support.

I cannot thank Jim and Debbie Cobrae enough for the friendship and support they have given us, for more than 15 years. I always look forward to our times together; you have truly been a friend. Thank you for introducing us to your friends and now ours in California, Bayless Conley and Tom Vialobos. Thank you for making the time and effort to help us build here in Zimbabwe. Rick Godwin is another of the significant voices that not only impacted Bonnie and me, but also spoke for many years prophetically into the nation of Zimbabwe. Rick, thank you for also introducing us to so many of your friends, Charles and Anne Stock; David Loveless, who has become a great friend and encourager, and Ron Corzine, who helped us with our newsletter in the USA. Of course, we were introduced to Alan and Eileen Vincent, who have left their fingerprints all over Africa with their great teaching ministry. Each of you has made the journey to Zimbabwe and has left a deposit here. I do not believe that any one of you has sown your life or ministry in vain. Wally and Marilyn Hickey made a memorable impact in the nation, once again highlighting the role of women in ministry. Betty Maltz, Bobbie Jean Merck, and scores of women from all around the world have raised the bar in this nation.

Jeff Perry and the teams of men led by his dad, "The General," can never be thanked enough for the role played in the building of our church building. You gave us hope; your spirits sustained ours when the length and the intensity of the battle had wearied us. You came with reinforcements and your help gave us courage to not only continue but to finish the task. Jeff, you have truly been a friend in deed as well as in word.

There are other friends whom we have met more recently, and although we have not known each other long, it seems as though we have been bound together with the cords of purpose. Randy and Renee Clark have been a constant source of encouragement and have partnered with our churches and family in creating a bigger worldview. Thank you for introducing us to Paul and Sandy Ward, who have become our dear friends. Wendell Smith has been a great encouragement, and has been influenced in great part once again by our friends Don and Marlene Ostrom.

Most recent are the relationships with men who are making a serious attempt to walk in the integrity that I have longed for since the day I started in the ministry. The Morningstar International world has welcomed me with open arms, and I am blessed to be associated with Rice Broocks, Phil Bonasso, Steve Murriel, Jim Laffoon, Brett Fuller, Greg Ball, Paul Daniels, and all the men and women of this truly international family.

If a building is built room-by-room, so are ministries. Bonnie and I realize that we are a sum of the parts of input that so many have poured into our lives. Although I have named so many people, my mind brings to focus so many more who have had a part to play in helping this story come to pass. I am sure that I have left out many significant names from this "Who's Who in the Life of Tom Deuschle." I am truly a rich man, and I do not want to take for granted any of the relationships that God has brought into my life. Not all of my relationships have borne fruit, nor are all of them still intact, whether through negligence, distance, time zones, misunderstandings, or conflict. I am persuaded that I am who I am because of the encounters with those whom God has brought into my life. I have been surprised at whom God will use, and how He uses both great and small, friend and foe, to mold our lives and make us who we are supposed to be.

I realize that through all my life experiences and relationships, I am one of the people whom God has built, and I am grateful to Him for letting me begin to build my dreams. I hope this book helps you to build your dreams, too.

Tom Deuschle
Harare, Zimbabwe
October 2002

CHAPTER 1

Where in the World Is Rhodesia?

Who in their right mind would move to a country in the middle of a brutal civil war—especially if they had few contacts there, no support from back home, and a wallet that was virtually empty?

That was how I landed in Zimbabwe—although when I arrived nearly 25 years ago, it was still called Rhodesia, and was one of the most lawless places on earth. I was not there because I was brave or had a sense of destiny on my life; in fact, I was racked by fear every step of the way. I was there because God had made it perfectly clear that Rhodesia was exactly where He wanted me.

The road to Rhodesia began in Denver, Colorado, where I was born in 1954. As the eldest of eight children in a Catholic family, I was naturally expected to become a priest. No one ever told me this, but it was an unspoken assumption that I would make the family very proud if I did. All the years of religious education and training taught me all about God, although I had no idea I could actually know Him—or indeed that I should know Him personally.

During the summer of 1971, my parents and siblings went to a Catholic retreat center near Taos, New Mexico. I was working a summer job and could not join them, but assumed that it would be like many of the other retreats we had gone to as a family. Imagine my shock when they returned to Denver completely changed. In fact, they made my life miserable for the next year, telling me I had to be baptized, that I needed to be filled with the Holy Spirit, and that I should be speaking in other tongues. They kept going to Catholic charismatic meetings that only seemed to fuel the fire in them—and their determination to ignite it in me, too.

Their persistence continued for a year, when I finally agreed to attend a Catholic charismatic Bible study. I listened intently as the speaker, who was a Presbyterian lay pastor, gave a challenging message on knowing Jesus. I realized I knew all *about* Him, but I did not *know* Him. For the first time in my life, I saw there was a difference. Six weeks later, in July 1972, I gave my life to Jesus. I told Him that I wanted to know Him personally, and I turned over control of my life to Him.

As I did, I had the clear impression that He was giving me marching orders. I'm not sure if it was an audible voice or a very deep impression, but I knew He was instructing me that I would serve Him in Rhodesia.

Rhodesia? I had heard of the place, but had no idea where it was, or why in the world God would tell me to go there. In fact, I had no interest in traveling—only making money and getting through school and on to university. So I filed "Rhodesia" in the back of my mind, and went about my new life with Jesus. I joined a Bible study that was started by some ex-hippies and drug addicts, and a year later when four of the leaders left, they told me, "We think you're supposed to lead the group now."

So as a one-year-old Christian, I started leading a Bible study. Seventy-five young people attended, and I promptly "grew" the group to thirty-five. Totally discouraged, I cried out to God. "You obviously made a mistake here," I told Him, "and these guys who asked me to lead did not know what they were talking about."

But God knew something I did not—including the fact that a spiritual explosion was about to take place at the high school my brothers and sisters attended. Within six months, 250 young people were born again—at a public high school—and began coming to my Bible study. Suddenly our little group became the most coveted of all the churches in town. When the members graduated, many went on to Bible school at Christ for the Nations (CFNI) in Dallas, Texas, and more than thirty of them eventually entered full-time ministry—most of them on the mission field.

I continued leading the Bible study after I enrolled at the University of Northern Colorado at Greeley, commuting to Denver every Thursday night. One of the courses I took at UNC during my junior year was a general education course—just to fill some credit hours that I needed. During the first class, the professor announced that he would not be teaching, but was instead turning over the course to an associate professor who had just returned from…Rhodesia.

The entire semester I sat under the conviction of the Holy Spirit. God began to speak to me in a peculiar way in every class as I felt a tug and pull toward this country whose name I had heard only a few years earlier. God's word to me was now beginning to take shape and meaning.

By the end of that year, I dropped out of my university courses, and enrolled at CFNI in Dallas. Somehow, students, instructors, and even guest lecturers constantly picked up on the fact that I was called to Africa—without my ever giving any indication of what the Lord had spoken to me. Being Catholic, I found the idea of missions a strange concept because I did not know how to go to a nation as a "missionary." All my Assembly of God friends would tell me to apply to a "mission board," but it did not seem right to apply to an organization where I had no relationship. Instead, I buried myself in ministry to which I could relate. I was a leader on campus, and organized many street outreaches, including a team of 160 young people who joined with Youth With A Mission to do an outreach in New Orleans during Mardi Gras. Our ministry was strong and direct, and in the mid-1970s was still considered cutting-edge and somewhat unpopular, but we felt God's hand on us as we ministered.

Ironically, I was painfully shy and almost insecure about my walk with God. I was not even sure of what I believed nor why I believed it. CFNI would host all of the charismatic guest speakers of the day, but I was actually more confused by the time I graduated than when I had arrived. I was not a particularly articulate speaker, but I had a gift of leadership in me—which only exacerbated my feelings of insecurity since I was a leader living in a speaker's world. As far as I could see, being a speaker was the best way to "minister."

When I graduated from CFNI, I signed up to go on a world tour with other CFNI students. We had heard that the Lord was doing great things all over the earth, and that people were being filled with the Holy Spirit—and quite frankly I wanted to see it for myself. I was thrilled not only to find out that it was true, but also to participate in this exciting move of God that was happening everywhere. We traveled throughout the Far East, the Middle East, and Europe—everywhere but Africa, which I seemed to be deftly avoiding. It was not that I was running from it; I just did not know what to do with the call that I had filed in the back of my mind. The more I tried to escape from the reality of going to Africa, the stronger the urgings became on my life. Yet whenever I tried talk to people about it, I got trite, simplistic answers in response. Everyone kept telling me I should be going to Africa, but I did not have a clue how to do it, or even why I should.

When the world tour was over, I had no clear direction of what I should do next, so I went back to Denver, where my dad and I started a family business—a greeting card distributorship. We started in our garage, working out of the trunk of our car, and barely made ends meet. We worked hard for little reward (although today the business has become very successful). To help supplement my income, a friend and I started another business hanging institutional draperies in hotels, hospitals, and apartment complexes. We were paid between $2 and $4 per bracket to hang them, which was a lot of money. Later we found out we could make even more by contracting with people to make the drapes for us. The business grew, and through it I was able to support many friends who were missionaries around the world.

I was settling into life—a good business, a girlfriend who seemed like the one God had sent me for life, and a house in Longmont, Colorado, that I had contracted to buy.

Yet there was that call in the back of my mind, and God wouldn't let me forget it. My life looked great on the outside, but inside I was confused and miserable. One night just after Christmas 1978, I came to the end of my rope. I was staying at my parents' home, and locked myself in one of the bedrooms to seek God. Basically I gave Him an ultimatum: If I did not hear from Him by the end of the year, I would marry my girlfriend, live in the house in Longmont, serve Him by leading Bible studies, and give up the whole crazy idea of going to Africa. It was December 27, so that gave Him just a few days to answer me.

It did not take Him nearly that long. At 6:00 the next morning, I woke up to my dad pounding on the locked bedroom door. I had fallen asleep on the floor where I had been calling out to God, and my arms and legs were almost im-mobilized from being in that position all night. My dad kept knocking, saying something about one of my friends calling from Dallas—and that they shouldn't be phoning that early in the morning. The voice at the other end of the phone was David Myers, whom I knew from the world tour. David had since gotten married, and we had lost touch. That morning he was calling me not from Dallas, as my dad thought, but from the other side of the world. David was calling me from Rhodesia. I had no idea that he had become a missionary to that country. That morning, he had been in a prayer meeting with other missionaries, including a young woman who knew me from the Bible study I had taught in college. She mentioned to David that I had a call on my life to go to Rhodesia, and he was now phoning to tell me they all felt I was supposed to join them.

"When are you going to come, Tom?" he asked me.

That was the sign I needed. I broke up with my girl-friend, let go of the option on the house, and gave my car to one brother and my furniture to another. On February 20, 1979, I headed for Africa—with one suitcase, a backpack, a guitar, $700, and return airfare.

CHAPTER 2

"He Came; He Cared; He Did Not Get Killed."

It was probably good that the Lord did not tell me too much about Rhodesia, or I might never have gone there. I knew the country was in the news, but I was unaware, for example, that Rhodesia was in the middle of a brutal civil war that threatened to tear the country apart. God had neglected to tell me about land mines, ambushes, food shortages, racial tensions, and the paralyzing fear that gripped the nation. He did not mention that there were international sanctions against the country, or that people were unable to buy the most common necessities. I did not know there was mandatory gasoline rationing, or that people could travel only during daylight hours because of curfews and police checkpoints on city streets. Nor did the Lord tell me that as a white man, I would not be welcomed by those who had been, in many instances, brutalized by whites.

He also forgot to inform me that before most missionaries ever set foot on foreign soil, they spend a year or two gathering financial support from friends, family, and churches back home. I had no support—and only $700 in my pocket. Nor did He tell me that most missionaries visit a country at least once before they decide to move there. I had successfully avoided Africa on my world tour a few years earlier and had no idea what was awaiting me when I did arrive.

God did not bother telling me any of this, nor a host of other things. Instead He was about to teach me about something much more valuable: the faithfulness of His character. What better place to learn about that than in an atmosphere of having to rely on Him—completely, totally, every moment of the day and night?

Faith, activated by hope, done in love, will produce a miracle.

As if I weren't stretched enough, God nearly succeeded in pulling me apart on my very first evening in Africa. The night I arrived, I went to a youth meeting in the Catholic Hall in the capital city of Salisbury (now called Harare), where 1,000 youth were listening to a former motorcycle-gang member give his testimony about how he met Jesus. I was jetlagged and could hardly stay awake, and stood in the back of the hall watching the scene as if it were a dream.

Suddenly I saw in my mind a picture of a lighthouse. There was no lighthouse in the hall, of course, but God was showing me something in the Spirit. Light streamed out of it, and as I watched, the light seemed to be coming out of Rhodesia itself—bands of light sweeping from the west to the east. God spoke to me and said, "This nation will be the springboard for the Gospel to go into the rest of Africa."

Then the picture changed, and I saw pinpricks of light bursting from Rhodesia—first one, then ten, twenty, a hundred—spilling out over the borders of Rhodesia going north-

ward. I saw the continent of Africa from the southern tip ignite with fire, which swept northward.

I had been in Rhodesia for barely a few hours. What in
the world was God saying to me, and how could He be
thinking that I might be a part of it?

Rhodesia was in the final days of its bloody civil war.
Until 1965, the country had been under British colonial
rule. At the time, the population was 8 million: 7.75 million
Africans and 250,000 Europeans (British, Dutch, and
French). In 1965, Britain wanted to cede rule to the
Africans and turn the country into an independent nation,
which delighted the Africans, who were in the vast majority.
The Europeans, however, had lived in Rhodesia for years,
built businesses, and raised families, and they had no intention of relinquishing their lives at the sweep of a pen.
Instead they declared a Unilateral Declaration of
Independence, known as UDI, and in defiance of Britain set
up their own government under the leadership of Ian Smith.
Britain responded by petitioning the United Nations, and as
a result Rhodesia became the first country with total world
economic sanctions against it. In fact, that was where U.N.
sanctions came into existence.

The civil war that followed was brutal on both sides. Just
two weeks before I arrived, a fuel depot in the heart of the
capital had been attacked, and fuel tanks blown up. The
Myers family, who had invited me to come to Africa, decided
the situation had gotten too dangerous for them to stay, and
they called me just before I left Denver. "If you're coming
because we've invited you to come," David had pointedly
told me, "don't, because we're leaving."

"You did not call me," I told him. "God did."

When I arrived in Rhodesia, I took over the rent on their
house. They gave me all their furniture, kitchen supplies,
and even their beat-up old Fiat. God was already restoring
what I had given away when I left Denver.

Because of the political situation in the country, I had a tremendous battle with fear. There was constant violence in the city, and every day people were attacked. I was living in a house all alone, and I was petrified to go out because of the gangs roaming the streets. I managed to leave the house long enough to fellowship at Mabelreign Chapel, the little church where David had attended. Some of the members had gone to CFNI, and as a result of my relationship with this church, I picked up where David had left off and began to minister at the African Bible College and later in the farming communities around the country.

In the midst of all the violence, I also ministered in public schools in a program called Right of Entry. The government of Rhodesia legislated that every schoolchild in the country had to receive one hour of religious instruction per week. Needless to say, this was a surprising doctrine to me, coming from the U.S. where we were busy banning all forms of prayer and religious education in schools. I knew it was God's opportunity to reach the young people of Rhodesia, and I taught 18 times a week and had the joy of leading many children to Christ. I had to study like mad in order to give a 30-minute message, however, because, frankly, I did not know anything. In fact, I was beginning to realize I was theologically bankrupt. Although I had been to Bible school, I really did not know what I believed. I came to Africa with notebooks filled with Bible studies, but when I taught people who were facing war and death on a daily basis, what I had to give them seemed trite and useless. How could they take my pat little teachings and act on them, when I was giving them nothing but fluff?

I started listening to a series of teaching tapes I got just before I left the States—by a Bible teacher named Fred Price. They were all about living by faith, and I nearly wore them out, listening to each tape over and over again. The

messages on those tapes, which were based solely and
solidly on the word of God, gave meaning to what I was
living. I realized that the only hope I could give to the
people I faced was the word of God, and Fred Price gave me
the assurance that the word of God was the word of God no
matter what the situation—whether exploding fuel depots in
Salisbury or broken families in Denver. I taught his messages almost verbatim for the first three months of my ministry life in Africa.

One of the tapes was on divine protection, and I began
to devour it—not just so that I could teach others, but also
because I needed it in my own life. I memorized the
Scriptures on the tape—Psalm 91 and Psalm 23 in particular:

He will cover you with his feathers,
And under his wings you will find refuge;
His faithfulness will be your shield and rampart.
You will not fear the terror of night,
Nor the arrow that flies by day,
Nor the pestilence that stalks in the darkness,
Nor the plague that destroys at midday.
A thousand may fall at your side,
Ten thousand at your right hand,
But it will not come near you (Psalm 91:4-7 NIV).

The Lord is my shepherd, I shall not be in want.
He makes me lie down in green pastures,
He leads me beside quiet waters,
He restores my soul.
He guides me in paths of righteousness
For his name's sake.
Even though I walk
Through the valley of the shadow of death,

I will fear no evil,
For you are with me (Psalm 23:1-4 NIV).

I was definitely in the valley of the shadow of death. I memorized these and a host of other Scriptures and began to confess the word of God in my own life. Sometimes it seemed as if it did little good because I was so fearful, but I kept on speaking God's Word. I had plenty of opportunity as I traveled through territory laced with land mines and ambushes. The old Fiat died, so I could not even hide inside that rusted piece of tin; instead I rode through the countryside first on a motorcycle and later in a bright yellow Datsun. Needless to say, I felt like a moving target.

God began to teach me tremendous lessons about trusting and obeying Him. During those early months, I taught at the African Bible College, and sometimes I would take my life in my hands just to get to class. Hostile gangs would occasionally come into the area, and if the students or instructors got wind of their presence in the vicinity or even on the campus, they would tie a red flag on the gate to warn me to stay away. If I saw that red flag, I did not stop, but would turn right around and head back home. I was white, and to the guerillas that meant I was the enemy—and they could easily have killed me on sight.

I also traveled to the white farms to speak with farmers. On many occasions, I found out after the fact that I had traveled through ambushes—and did not even know it. On at least two occasions I was actually fired on; I never knew it, but others told me about it later. Twice I traveled over stretches of roads planted with landmines, yet they never went off. I began to learn to hear the voice of the Holy Spirit; once He clearly directed me to take a certain road, and I obeyed, even though it was ten kilometers longer than the regular route. I later learned that the road I would have taken was mined, and a tractor driving on it was blown up as it crossed a bridge. The next time I went back to that farm, 300 people were waiting in a hall to hear me speak. The story had gotten out all over the community about this crazy American. "He came, he cared, and he did not get killed," they said, and they wanted to hear about the God I served.

Yet the fear plaguing me never let up. One night I was in bed when I heard a mortar go off. Up until that point, the freedom fighters had never actually shot mortars in the city itself, so this was a significant breach of security. I was petrified and nearly paralyzed with fear. Another mortar went off, and then another, flying right over my home and landing on a golf course nearby. Any one of them could have easily landed on my house. Some of the mortars were not even primed; they landed on the golf course without going off, meaning there were live rounds of ammunition that could explode at any moment.

As I was lying in bed absolutely terrified, all I could do was quote Scriptures—Psalm 23, Psalm 91, and all the others I had memorized. Suddenly something broke in my heart, and just as I was quoting 2 Timothy 1:7—"For God has not given us a spirit of fear, but of power and of love and of a sound mind" (NKJ)—I saw a picture in my mind of a giant angel standing over my house. He was holding a baseball bat, and as I lay there listening to the sound of mortars whistling overhead, I watched that angel actually hitting home runs with the mortars!

At that moment, the overwhelming fear that had so paralyzed me broke off my life and never bothered me again. God had used the truth of His Word to deliver me, and I learned a powerful lesson that night. We can confess all the Scriptures we want, but when someone is trying to kill us, we have to get hold of God for ourselves and know the absolute truth of His Word—that if He says He is going to protect us, then He will protect us. I reached that point that night, and from then on I knew beyond any doubt that God's hand was on me. It was a turning point in my life, and I have seen God's divine protection on me ever since.

About the same time that I learned that lesson about God's character, my finances dried up. The pittance that I had when I arrived in Africa—all of $700—lasted about three months, and I had no clue where more would come from. I went to my mailbox at least twice a day hoping God would speak to someone to help me. I began writing pleading, begging letters back home, thinking that is what missionaries should do. A trickle came in, but my rent was Z$85 (about US$180 at the time). I soon came to the end of my money and was about to go into debt.

I decided that it was time for another dialogue with God. I felt strongly that He was telling me to "fast" from looking in my mailbox for 30 days. I realized that my mailbox had become my source and provider. God also seemed to be saying if I would make my needs known to Him and trust Him for my finances, He would provide.

I told no one about any of this, and as far as my friends knew, all my needs were met and I had plenty of money. Meanwhile, I was nearing the thirtieth day of my fast and was now one month behind in my rent. About the only thing that happened during this time was that two young women left some bags of groceries for me—significant, but not enough to pay my bills or cover my rent.

At the time, I was teaching a Bible study to about a dozen people. We met in my home, where we studied Derek Prince's "Foundation" series. One night after everyone went home, I was putting away my guitar, and in the place where I kept the guitar picks and straps, I noticed an envelope. When I opened it, I was amazed to discover Z$1,200 tucked inside—about US$2,600. To this day, I have no idea how it got there. It was a tremendous amount of money, and a powerful sign of God's provision for me.

From that time onward, God has led me to trust Him completely for the finances to do His work, both personally and for the ministry. I watched Him continually do amazing things to supply my needs. Once when I was in the U.S. on furlough, I taught a Bible study in a small church. One of the men interrupted me in the middle of it and said, "Are you believing God for an airplane?" As a matter of fact, I had been confessing and believing, and had put a picture of a plane on my refrigerator in Africa. The man told me he had just come into an inheritance, and he gave me what I needed to buy the plane—US$28,000. I went back to Africa and bought a Piper Cherokee Archer. That same plane today would cost US$200,000.

Learning to trust God to provide was another lesson I learned from those teaching tapes by Fred Price. I noticed that he kept mentioning a "Brother Hagin." I had no idea who he was, but assumed he must be someone special. Later that year, I met Pastor Ray McCauley who had just started a church in South Africa. Ray had recently graduated from Rhema Bible School in Tulsa, Oklahoma, headed by the very same "Brother Hagin." Ray very graciously gave me a complete set of Kenneth Hagin's books and tapes—and I had new material to devour. The teachings became the foundation of my belief system, and as I learned it, I taught it. I got my hands on everything I could find from what was known as the faith movement, and it became the basis of my ministry.

God was giving me the keys to His Kingdom. Before I came to Africa, I had been teaching nice little Bible studies, but people who were being mortared and attacked needed answers to the hard questions they were facing on a daily basis—how to survive a war, how to live in divine health, how to walk in God's protection, and how to feed their families in the midst of a civil war and international economic sanctions.

As God was shaping my ministry, He was also shaping me. In fact, there was more of the latter going on than anything else. He showed me that my ministry was not what I did; it was what I became. God pointedly told me that He was not interested in what I could do for Him. He wanted to minister to others through me, and it was important to Him what I became in the process of teaching His truths.

He continued shaping me, sometimes in painful ways. Although I had learned how to trust God for protection and provision, I was still agonizingly shy and insecure. It seemed as if I would die a million deaths if I had to get up and speak—and there was plenty of opportunity for that. As soon as God poured His anointing on me, I was fine, but until that happened, I was a wreck. Somehow the Lord managed to use me to start churches all over the country, including six in the rural districts. I had many friends, both black and white, in these churches and at the African Bible College where I continued to teach.

I also bought a small house for Z$14,000. Since I was traveling a lot, I invited another missionary family to live in the house with me. I covered the mortgage, and they covered water and electricity. I was never alone, but ironically I felt lonely.

I had no idea how isolated I could feel living in a war-torn nation. Many of my friends and neighbors were planning to leave but wouldn't tell anyone. They called it "taking the gap," and all of a sudden they would have everything ready and announce they were leaving. It did not matter that I had developed a friendship with them; they would be gone. Others simply disappeared, and when I inquired about them, I was told they had taken the gap. It was painful, and it only seemed to get worse.

Worse than this pain was the one resulting from the excruciating work that God began to do in my heart—which nearly devastated me. He showed me that I had not only accommodated some of the racist attitudes of foreigners living in Rhodesia, but that I had actually adopted some of these attitudes myself. One leader whom I worked with had such bitterness in his heart toward the African people that he had to leave the country. God began to show me that some of his attitudes had crept into my own heart, and that I needed to separate myself from all the people I had been ministering with in that particular movement. I went through a painful process of unbundling myself and breaking off the soul ties with these people. Most of them eventually left the country, but it was a very agonizing process at the time to meet with them, clarify my position, and break off the relationship.

In one particularly difficult instance, I yielded my rights to my airplane. I had bought the plane, but another missionary paid for my flight training in exchange for the right to use it. I no longer had enough need or finance to continue flying after the civil war stopped, so I gave up my rights to the plane. It was not giving up the plane that was painful, but breaking the relationship with this man—and that was just one of many. It broke me so badly that I decided to fly to South Africa with Ray McCauley. I spent three days in his guest room, agonizing over what I was going through. It was like open-heart surgery as God showed me what was really in my heart—attitudes and "baggage" that had to go if I was going to stay and minister for Him in Africa.

One of the attitudes concerned the economic sanctions that we all lived with. It had become standard operating procedure—even for missionaries—to get around the sanctions however necessary, with the excuse that we were doing the Lord's work. If we had to lie, cheat on customs, or smuggle things into the country, we rationalized that it was all right. In fact, if you got around the sanctions, you were almost looked upon as a hero. It was an attitude rewarded by the ministers and leaders of the city, particularly the group I was with. I knew I could no longer participate in that kind of activity.

God also did an attitude adjustment in me toward the spirit that says, "God loves Rhodesia." I had gotten into big trouble over this from day one, because I could not accept it, so I confronted it whenever I could. My response was, "God doesn't love Rhodesia. God doesn't love America. He'll bless any nation that aligns itself with His laws and His Kingdom. But any nation that thinks it will be blessed because of its own sovereignty is mistaken. God has no obligation to a country—only to His Word."

That was not a popular sentiment, and still is not, especially in the United States. It put me in conflict with many of the preachers of the day who were saying that God was for a pro-white Rhodesia. I worked with many of the African Bible College students, and heard them pray prayers for their brothers and sisters fighting a war against the colonial oppression. I also had many friends among the white farmers who regularly faced terrorism by the guerillas. Neither one of the positions was right theologically, but the people who espoused them were sincere—sincerely wrong. I remember seeing a cartoon by Charles Shultz of Charlie Brown and Snoopy on a baseball field. They were disheveled and had obviously lost the game. The caption read, "How could we lose when we were so sincere?" This is how I saw my brothers and sisters on both sides of the issue: sincere but at a loss for real answers to the problems they were facing.

Ironically many of the European people and leaders fled to South Africa and were faced with the issue again there during the dismantling of apartheid. I once heard Bob Mumford refer to this as "having to go around the mountain again." God will teach us His lessons, and we will learn them regardless of the geographical location where we move ourselves.

I also found myself confronting the attitude of white superiority over blacks. Many missionaries got around this by saying that white people had a superiority over blacks because they had lived privileged lives, which somehow made them better. They weren't necessarily saying that whites were genetically or innately superior to blacks simply because of their color, but they used the excuse of privilege to justify their racism. It was hard for them to embrace an uneducated and uncivilized black from a rural area because his or her customs and manners were so un-western. So rather than seeing that person as having any value, many in the white culture generalized their attitude by saying, "All blacks are like this," or "The blacks have this or that problem."

Not surprisingly, the war's atrocities resulted in hatred on both sides, creating a thinking that expressed itself in stereotypical language and statements. For example, it was common to see posters showing a black man and a white woman holding hands, walking away from the camera. The caption was, "Is this what you want?" It might as well have said, "If we give them independence, this is what you'll get." That offended me, and I guess I was not wise enough to keep my mouth shut. I would ask other whites, "Do you believe this?" The danger of that line of thinking is that many people became eurocentric and saw everything through European eyes, becoming critical and judgmental of anyone who was not a white European.

The deep wounds that divided the country did not automatically heal when the new nation of Zimbabwe was born on April 18, 1980—nor was there an end to the painful time of open-heart surgery that God was performing on me. Even after independence, He continued revealing to me how racist beliefs had crept into my own soul and way of thinking. He seemed to shine a flashlight into the very corners of my heart, showing me that I had adopted these attitudes. Whether I had done so consciously or unconsciously, I was in danger of being marginalized. It was the dawn of a new day, and if I was going to work in Zimbabwe, God had to take me through a much-needed breaking process.

At times, it was so cataclysmic that I thought I was going to die. I was breaking friendships that had been my life source, and changing thought patterns that I did not realize were so deeply rooted. To tear them out meant tearing out a part of me, but I knew they had to go.

I felt it was time to go back to the United States for a furlough, but as I was about to leave Zimbabwe, the Lord gave me one more giant opportunity to trust Him. I received word that one of the other pastors in the country had filed papers that would declare me a Prohibitive Immigrant. If his petition was successful, it would mean I could never return to Zimbabwe.

I was devastated, not only at the thought of being kept away from the country I had adopted as my own, but also because one of my own brothers—a fellow Christian—was trying to keep me out. I supposed I had ruffled too many feathers.

Not knowing what else to do, I got on a plane and headed for "home." My real home, of course, was the one I was leaving—the beautiful land that drew further and further away as I pressed my head against the window of the plane. I felt like a man without a country. Would I ever see Zimbabwe again?

CHAPTER 3

Bonnie

" The Lord says, 'I will be the fire round about you.'"
I did not know the man who spoke these words to
me, but I wanted to tell him that he had no idea
how true they were. Since I had returned to the United
States just a few days earlier, the fire raging about me had
not let up. I was thousands of miles from Zimbabwe, but the
scorch marks seemed as fresh as ever.

Now a stranger was telling me that God Himself was the
fire round about me. The stranger was Dick Mills, a Bible
teacher who was speaking at a seminar at Christ for the
Nations that I decided to attend not long after I returned to
the States. Dick had pulled me out of the crowd and started
prophesying to me. Of course, he had no idea who I was,
where I had just come from, or that I was indeed in the
midst of a major fire.

His words to me were straight out of the book of
Zechariah: "I will be the fire round about you," he said. But
then it got better: "I will be the glory in the midst of you,"
he continued, quoting from Zechariah 2:5. "Young man, no
one will be able to touch you or harm you," he said, adding
that I should not fear what any man had done to me and
that I should be willing to go back to the city that God had

called me from because no one would be able to hurt me. Then he quoted from Acts 18:9-10: "The Lord spoke to Paul in a vision: 'Do not be afraid; keep on speaking, do not be silent. For I am with you, and no one is going to attack and harm you, because I have many people in this city'" (NIV). Dick did not miss a beat. "I don't know what happened to you, young man," he continued, "but someone has risen up against you and tried to block you. But God says you're not to worry. You're to return, and He will prosper and bless you."

I could not have a clearer mandate to return to Zimbabwe than if God Himself had handed me stone tablets and a return plane ticket. I had no idea what God was up to, but I returned to the apartment where I was staying, fell on my face, and wept. "God, You must know something," I told Him. "I trust You."

I needed someone to talk to, and was glad that my good friend Larry Hill was due to be at the same CFNI seminar. We had known each other when we were students at CFNI, and had ministered together on many occasions. Larry was now a missionary to Mexico, and I knew he would understand what I was going through. The only problem was that he had not arrived at the seminar yet. He was still in Kansas, held up by a massive flood that had hit the state.

Finally he pulled into Dallas on Wednesday evening, along with his girlfriend who had driven down from Kansas with him. I planned to meet both of them after the evening service. The meeting that night was powerful, and I remember a young woman singing a song so anointed that the entire crowd erupted into a standing ovation of praise. I was dumbfounded not only at the range of her voice, but at her anointing and beauty.

When I met Larry after the service, I learned that this singer was his girlfriend—Bonnie Laughlin. The three of us went to dinner after the service, and Larry and I caught up on everything that had happened since we had last been together. This was only the second time I had been back in the States since I moved to Africa, so I desperately needed someone to talk to. Larry was a real friend, and listened as I unloaded the pain in my heart. I don't know what Bonnie thought of all my grievances, but she probably told the Lord that she never wanted to become a missionary or set foot in Africa.

Later in the week, Larry had to fly back to Mexico, so Bonnie and I drove him to the Dallas-Fort Worth airport. As we said goodbye, Larry asked me, "Tom, would you take care of Bonnie for me?"

"She's your girlfriend," I told him, feeling somewhat uncomfortable at his request, but I grudgingly told him that I would take Bonnie to dinner.

For the next two weeks, I was busy itinerating, and when I eventually returned to CFNI, I phoned the assistant dean of women and asked if she would like to go to dinner with Larry's girlfriend and me. I kept it all on the up and up. After all, I was a righteous man and Larry's friend!

I was scheduled to speak at a church the following weekend, and it turned out that Bonnie was supposed to sing at the same service, so we decided to drive there together. During the Saturday evening service, I was in the middle of teaching a Bible study, when someone interrupted me and—in what seemed to be a pattern for my ministry—started prophesying to me. Her words absolutely shocked me: "God shows me that you two are going to get married," she said.

I quickly interrupted and shut down her prophecy. "Thank you," I said, "but God hasn't shown me that."

Bonnie and I ministered the next morning and evening, without benefit of any more prophetic words, and we just seemed to flow together. On the drive back to Dallas, I asked what her relationship was with Larry. When she said she had broken up with him, I asked if I could pursue a relationship with her, and she said yes.

We saw each other the next night and the night after that. I did not know it at the time, but Bonnie had already phoned her mother and said, "I think I'm getting married."

"To Larry?" her mother asked. It was a logical question because Bonnie had just been visiting her mother with Larry.

"No," Bonnie said. "To Tom."

"Tom who?"

"I don't know."

"Well, how do you know him?" her mother pressed. "Where does he live?"

"He's from Africa."

"Africa! What color is he?"

Bonnie had a lot of friends from Ghana, and her mother just assumed I was one of them. On Wednesday evening, Bonnie and I went to the home of some of her friends, and it was very clear they did not like me. In fact, they liked Larry. The four of us prayed together, and I felt God speak to my heart. That night I asked Bonnie to marry me, and she said yes. We had known each other for just three days.

Three months later we were married, two weeks after that we flew to Africa, and six months later we started a church.[2]

Being a missionary, a pastor's wife, and living in Africa were the furthest things from Bonnie's mind when she was growing up. In fact, while her roommates at CFNI fasted and prayed over foreign countries, waiting to hear God's call to go to the mission field, Bonnie poured her life into her music ministry. The eldest of two daughters, she had a keen ear for music and won several state awards for her singing. She learned to play piano, French horn, and trumpet, and began writing her own songs at the age of twelve.

After she graduated from high school, she became a member of Fred Waring's "Pennsylvanians" and traveled with the group, gaining valuable professional experience. She was headed for a lucrative and public career—yet she knew something was missing in her life. One day she heard the testimony of Debbie Barns Miles who was Miss America 1967, about how she had found Jesus. In response, Bonnie gave her life to the Lord and dedicated her music career to Him.

She went back to school, enrolling at Oral Roberts University, where she was accepted as one of a group of ten artists known as the World Action Singers. She went on tour extensively throughout the United States with Richard Roberts and the World Action Singers, and appeared weekly on Oral Roberts' Sunday morning television program. She graduated with an honors degree in music education, and finally enrolled at CFNI in Dallas for further Bible training, including an extensive study of praise and worship.

This professional singer—who had two music degrees, who had performed at the Grand Ol' Opry, who wrote songs that were eventually recorded by Integrity Music and other international music companies, who was being courted by Christian music companies to become the next Evie—gave it all up to move to Africa with me. She traded working with some of the top professionals in the world, for singing in a country that did not even have an adequate sound system. In fact, the first time we ministered together in Zimbabwe, her "sound engineer" was a local auto mechanic. She gave him a hand signal to raise the volume, and he put his ear next to the speaker, smiled, and nodded to her that it was working.

Bonnie called it her "signs-and-wonder" ministry; she would make a sign and everyone would wonder what she meant.

Our first year together in Zimbabwe was a time of great adjustment for Bonnie in other areas too. She went through culture shock, ministry shock, and marriage shock being joined to someone she barely knew in a country she did not know at all. But the clear mandate we both had from God kept us going. From the beginning, we were willing to work through every issue in our lives. We were both the first born in our families, and were both strong leaders and strong willed, but God knew that it would take a special pair to be able to pioneer what He wanted to do in Africa.

I came from a family of six boys and two girls with plenty of male hormones to spare; Bonnie came from a broken home of two girls who read poetry and played dress-up, with no male hormones to spare. Somehow God blended our lives together, and from day one, our life in Africa was filled with intense fellowship. I immediately tried to bring Bonnie into my world of airplanes, travel, harsh living conditions, and a different ministry venue every night—a constant array of new faces and new friends. I could not understand why she could not adapt in a few weeks when it had taken me three years to adjust.

I will never forget the look in her eyes as I left her at a bus stop with two French-speaking Mauritians, who were settler farmers and close friends of mine, along with a crowd of people who had nothing else to do but watch a young woman cry. I was on my way to South Africa to buy a motorcycle for myself (under the guise of needing it for ministry), and I left Bonnie to spend her first Christmas in Africa without me—in 100° Fahrenheit heat, no turkey and dressing but cold meats and salad, and everyone wearing swim suits. It sounded like a reasonable plan to me, but four days later when I returned, I was met by a young wife whom

I had wounded deeply without even knowing what I had done wrong. The scars of neglect that I inflicted were not the only ones she bore. The very first woman to greet my new wife was a pastor's wife. When she heard that Bonnie had been a beauty queen (Miss Tulsa and homecoming queen at Oral Roberts University), she felt that it was her responsibility to announce that Bonnie's American ways and all of her makeup, hairstyles, and fancy clothes were not wanted or needed in Zimbabwe. She was quite emphatic that Bonnie herself would not be received if she did not simplify her ways.

Bonnie's strong character and outspoken ways, which I had so admired, were not well received in a strong male-dominated society, where most women used their gifts, skills, and education only if they did not challenge a man's world. The fact that I saw Bonnie as my equal and released her to lead with all of her gifts brought heavy criticism and many personal challenges both from men and women. Needless to say, the Zimbabwean culture (both European and African) was not receptive to strong female leadership. Once again the deficiencies in my own character often left my wife fending for herself and fighting battles that I should have taken as part of my headship in the home. For many years these were painful experiences, with painful lessons that I needed to learn. Unfortunately, it took a great toll on Bonnie's effervescent and outgoing personality (in every competition and at every school she ever attended, she was always Miss Congeniality).

Bonnie's deep faith in God and her commitment to me were unwavering, and she always rose above every challenge. I will never forget the first letter she wrote home to her family. It aptly described many of the feelings and challenges she was facing in her first few months in Africa.

January 19, 1982
Dear Friends,

Greetings from deep dark Africa! I have been wanting to write to you and to let you know that Tom and I are surviving. Actually we are flourishing and blessed!...Tom and I live in a beautiful three-bedroom house on an acre and one-tenth of land. It is a white Spanish-style house with a concrete scalloped fence...The house is very modern and well built and if I did not know any better I would still think I was in America. There are, however, a few slight differences. The windows have no screens so if you want fresh air you learn to live with bugs, and you do want the doors open as there are no air conditioners or heaters in any of the houses. We do have permanent house spiders that live on our walls the year round. In some areas people have lizards living on their walls. I have learned not to be squeamish any more!...We have a gas stove, a small refrigerator, and hot and cold running water! No one has a garbage disposal or trash compacter, a microwave or a Mr. Coffee. But we have a Sweeney!

The general pace of the country is much slower and simpler than America. Most of the stores remind me of small grocers years ago with a butcher and baker next door. There are no McDonalds, Burger Kings, Taco Bells, Baskin Robbins, Sambos, diet soda, or Pizza Huts. There are no cake mixes, Hamburger Helpers, or TV dinners. The bread is unwrapped and unsliced for 25¢ a loaf...There is only one milk. No two percent, one percent, low fat, vitamin D added, buttermilk, skimmed, chocolate, etc., just milk...It comes either in a plastic sack in the store or in bottles from the milkman. We eat mostly fresh fruit and vegetables, although there are some canned....

Basically there exist two different cultures living side by side. The first is the white European. These people are very British and proud. They love their hot tea with milk, which I am beginning to enjoy, and every hour on the hour is tea time!..Like the British they drive on the left-hand side of the street, which took me quite a while to catch on to. The first time I drove I felt like an accident looking for a place to happen...I had to concentrate so hard on staying on the left that I would forget to shift. What made it worse was that the shift is on the left, as the steering wheel is on the right. I could not shift into third gear so I had to go very slowly. Secondly the turn signal and the headlight switch were opposite from what I'm used to. By mistake I would hit the light switch, which confused the people behind me and when I would hit the turn signal I would hit the right signal and turn left. The motorists behind me kept passing and hooting (what they call for honking). Tom got a real laugh out of that one. Now, however, I am getting quite used to it and can finally enjoy driving...

The second main culture in Zimbabwe is the black African. Steeped in years of tribal life and ancestral worship, these people are very strong, good natured, [and] fun loving...Gradually these people have taken over the country as it has changed from a white to a black-rule government. There are seventy blacks to one white. It makes me feel like a marshmallow in hot chocolate!...These people are very skilled with their hands. Women make beautiful knitted and crocheted clothing and doilies. They make beautiful handbags, wicker baskets, and carvings. [For the most part] they do not have a concept of time, however, and it is nothing for one of them to be two hours late, which makes for an unstable economy. There are two major tribal factions here, which in turn are broken up into many tribes and they are very loyal to their chiefs. They keep their traditions and customs and still buy their wives with lobola (money or cattle)...I have learned much about the Africans from our domestic worker, Sweeney.

Sweeney is 65 years old...He is very thin, rather short,

with white crooked teeth and a shy laugh. He calls Tom "boss" and me "madam," and he cooks, cleans, makes beds, does dishes, works on the lawn, and does the laundry. He is such a nice spirited person to have working for us...Of course I do get my share of the work as he is off for two days at a time and when he is here he cannot be everywhere at once, so I do the dishes, make the beds and cook quite often. We also have a constant flow of people through our home, so I've called this the Deuschle Hotel! Without Sweeney it would be frantic. Since he was trained by a British woman, he does not know all the American dishes like our pizza, so I cook them. He has an excellent memory, is a fabulous chef, and is quite a character. He makes the best scrambled eggs this side of the equator and serves us with a towel draped over his arm. Real class! He is not always really neat as he gets the bedspreads crooked quite often and he misses cobwebs and dust, but I do not mind. I enjoy having him here especially when Tom is gone...Although Tom is very businesslike with him, Sweeney and I have become good buddies (sometimes he even tells me what to do)...

Recently Tom's brother Bob and a friend Jeff came to visit us for 60 days, and we took [time] off to see the country, travel in the bush, and sleep in mud huts with them...With Bob and Jeff reacting to the cultural differences here, I can see how I have already adapted to the life here. The most important thing that I have learned so far is to be content with whatever situation I am in (Philippians 4:11). I have learned not to take so much for granted and to realize how blessed we really are. For instance, in America if I had some moldy cheese I would throw it away. Now because it is so scarce we scrape the mold off and eat it no matter what its condition.

My vision for God's world has expanded as I see how big

God is and how vast His world. Yet He is the same every-where! It is amazing to hear the African people speak of the same Jesus and the power of God that I knew in America. Tom and I see a tremendous need to teach the people, whites and blacks, and we have already seen many people saved, blessed, healed, filled with the Spirit, delivered and set free by the power of God. It's exciting! It is a challenge to be used by God to meet people's needs. I praise Him for the experience and privilege of being here…Just a few days ago we ministered at a large black African tent revival meeting where we needed an interpreter for the Shona-speaking Africans. After listening to them sing in ten-part harmony, watching their simple child-like faith, and seeing them listen intently seated on a straw floor, I knew I was in Africa. It was like watching a National Geographic special on TV…

It is a challenge to be used by God to meet people's needs and to teach them to live a victorious Christian life through the power of His Word. I praise Him for the experience and privilege of being here.

Love,
Bonnie

CHAPTER 4

Word, Work,
Wonders, and Warfare

When Bonnie and I began our life together in Zimbabwe, the economy was still suffering from years of economic sanctions, and there were extreme shortages of even basic commodities such as toothpaste, toilet tissue, and other necessities. It was a very harsh environment to even think about raising a family. Before I married, my ministry had been evangelistic—traveling and speaking all over the country and in South Africa. When Bonnie and I began traveling and ministering as a couple, God seemed to give us great favor, and we wondered if we were supposed to be based in South Africa. It seemed like a logical possibility for many reasons. It was a much more secure place to raise a family, and there was more opportunity for both of us, especially for Bonnie's worship ministry. South Africa was really a first-world country with a third-world population. It had every benefit of first-world living, and each time we would go there, we would satisfy all our physical desires—chocolate, diet Cokes, tuna fish, cheese, dried fruit, toothpaste, light bulbs, and all those things that missionaries feel they cannot live without. South Africa was growing on us.

One night in April 1982, we were in the midst of a ministry tour there, and after our own evening meeting we decided to drop by a meeting at Ray McCauley's Rhema Church. By the time we arrived, Ray was well into his message, so we quietly found seats on the back row. In the middle of the message, Ray stopped, looked at Bonnie and me, and told us to stand up. In a voice that seemed to go right through me, he began prophesying to us.

"God is telling you to turn 180 degrees from the way you are going," he said. "You're to fast and pray during the next three days, and He will reveal to you, like you are seeing it on a television screen, an open vision of what you are supposed to do."

We did not like that word for a number of reasons. First, we knew that turning 180 degrees meant going back to Zimbabwe, which we had pretty much decided to leave at that point. Second, the idea of fasting in South Africa was a real sacrifice because we were frankly enjoying all the good food and amenities.

But of course we listened to God, and fasted and prayed during our remaining days in South Africa. True to His word, God spoke clearly and said we should return to Zimbabwe and plant a strong Word-based church in Harare, which was to meet the needs of people—spirit, soul, and body—and if we would do that, whatever we laid our hand to He would bless and prosper. And there was more: He said this church would also provide a base of operation to organize an effective outreach to the rest of Zimbabwe as well as the five surrounding nations of central Africa.

That mandate was clear, and we knew it was from the Lord.

The night we arrived back home and pulled into our driveway, two men were sitting on the veranda. They walked over to us and said, "God spoke to us and said you were starting a church. We're the first two members."

Of course, we had told no one of our plans. That was a Saturday night. The next morning, the two men returned to our house with their families, and we started our church— the two couples, their children, Bonnie, and me. Bonnie led praise and worship, then ran out and took care of the children. I taught a Bible study, we both made tea, and by the time everyone left, we were absolutely exhausted. I could not imagine doing more, and wondered what God was thinking of asking us to start a church.

Ray offered the name "Rhema" to us, which was the name of his church in Johannesburg, and I eagerly accepted the offer. Two months later, we rented an auditorium in the suburb of Mount Pleasant, and on June 6, 1982, we had our first official service as Rhema Bible Church with 52 people in attendance. The stage was old and dusty, but I invited anyone who needed healing to come up for prayer. A woman whose body was filled with blood clots came forward, as did a man with chronic back and neck problems. I prayed for them, and they both fell onto the dirty stage. We did not even know that we should have someone waiting to catch them. They landed in a heap on the dirty stage as a cloud of dust rose up around them. I had never seen anything like it. To our great astonishment, God healed both of them that day.

The church continued to grow, and by August we knew we needed a permanent location. We had started the church only 14 weeks earlier, but God was bringing the increase, and we had to work hard to keep up with Him. We learned about an old hotel that was on the market. The owner had tried to sell it three or four times, only to have it returned because the buyers could not make payments or reneged on the loan. He was asking Z$250,000, but said he would sell it to us for Z$120,000, which at the time was about one-to-one with the U.S. dollar.

I told him we'd take it. Of course, we had no money, and
no logical place to look for it. I gathered 14 men together
from the church, and said we needed Z$120,000. Together
we came up with Z$6,000—far short of even the Z$12,000
we needed for the ten percent down payment. On the day
the Z$6,000 was due, I had no choice but to tell the real es-
tate agent that we had only half the money, and ask if we
could work out a deal. I had no idea where the rest of the
money would come from, but I was trying to buy some time.

As I walked to the real estate agent's office, a car pulled
to a stop right in the middle of an intersection, and the
driver jumped out, waving and yelling at me. "I've been
looking all over for you," he called. Right there, in the
middle of the intersection, he pulled out his checkbook, and
on the hood of his car wrote out a check for Z$6,000—and
we had our down payment.

The building became the "nerve center" for the ministry, with plenty of space not only for midweek services,
but also for offices, counseling rooms, a bookstore and tape
library, a youth ministry, children's church and Bible
school. At first, the handful of people rattled around in the
offices and in the 170-seat meeting hall, but each week
more and more came for the ministry we offered. We continued to hold services in the Mount Pleasant Hall, also, and
our numbers began to swell with many curious onlookers
showing up as well. The Holy Spirit showed up, too—with
signs and wonders. Whenever I prayed for people, without
even touching them, they fell in the Spirit, and many were
healed, delivered, and filled with the Holy Spirit. The
church became known for this "signs-and-wonders" ministry, and even more people came, particularly non-
Christians who had never seen anything like this before.

Our goal was to reach out to those who did not know
Jesus; we did not want to "steal sheep," a term that referred

to luring away members of another church. In fact, when we started our church, I even wrote letters to all the pastors in the city announcing our plans, and we did not receive any negative responses. As our church grew, however, the city's seven leading charismatic and Pentecostal pastors called me to a special meeting and grilled me for two hours. They said what I was doing was of the devil and was dividing the body of Christ.

Their reaction devastated me and broke my heart, and I went into a deep despair and depression. Bonnie and I could not fathom what had happened or what we had done to deserve such a vicious attack. We had dutifully informed every pastor of the city in writing (and some even in person) of our intention to start a church, and no one seemed to object. It was only after our church began to experience remarkable growth that the accusations began to fly.

Looking back, we were pioneering a message of healing, prosperity, and faith, and in those days there was a lot of resistance to that message. The church was growing, but the persecution was agony. Almost all the pastors in town eventually opposed us and spoke against us from their pulpits. They labeled us a prosperity and healing cult. Others said we were a church that catered to the wealthy, and that you had to drive a Mercedes to attend our church. Some said we told people to throw away their medicine and "believe God for a healing"—something we would never counsel. Still others told their congregations that we charged money for our services, and if you did not pay a certain amount, you could not come.

Civil war in the nation had ended, but this war within the church seemed almost as devastating. The vocal opposition only served to advertise our meetings, however, and many people came simply out of curiosity. Then we were accused of stealing sheep. If anything, we were not sheep stealers but sheep feeders; people were hungry for more, and we served a good spiritual meal. At the time, the largest church in the city had 400 members. We were growing rapidly, and already had 150 members. Most of these were new converts, which is whom we were after, although there were some transfers. The growth was unprecedented—and apparently threatening—and the persecution wounded Bonnie and me deeply.

At that critical time, I remembered something that a friend told me when I began in the ministry: "Any vision that is worthy of heaven will suffer an attack from hell." In my naiveté back then, I had no idea what he was talking about, and although I had studied spiritual warfare from a textbook and had been to many prayer meetings, it was not until we launched our church that I experienced real spiritual warfare. Unfortunately I also did not understand from which direction it would come. Sometimes the attack comes from those we do not expect, and it wounds deeply when it comes from within the body of Christ.

The leading charismatic pastor of the city contacted Freda Lindsay, president of Christ for the Nations, the Bible school that I had attended in Dallas. There were a number of CFNI graduates in Zimbabwe, and since this pastor was the CFNI representative in the city, he felt Mrs. Lindsay should know that I was, in his words, dividing the church. And so a few months after the grilling public opposition that I had received from the local pastors, Mrs. Lindsay paid a visit to the city. In front of 52 Christ for the Nations graduates, she chastised and blackballed Bonnie and me, saying we were the source of division in the churches of the nation.

Sadly, Mrs. Lindsay did not talk to me before she made her public statements. I made many requests to speak to her privately so that she could hear my side of the story, but she refused to speak to me, heeding only the counsel of this leader.[3]

For the next ten years, there was a constant barrage of

accusation leveled against us from every quarter. We were branded a cult and a Harvard professor even wrote a book that labeled us part of the religious right of America and lumped us together with the likes of the "Moonies" and Billy Graham, the latter of whom I count it a privilege to be associated with.

During these difficult times, Romans 5:3-5 ministered deeply to both Bonnie and me: "We also rejoice in our sufferings, because we know that suffering produces perseverance; perseverance, character; and character, hope. And hope does not disappoint us, because God has poured out his love into our hearts by the Holy Spirit, whom he has given us" (NIV).

Perseverance will always outlast persecution.

Through the trials we faced, we began to understand that suffering comes into our lives to teach us perseverance, and perseverance builds godly character, and when left to run its full course will create hope. God was "working all things together for his good" in our lives in the midst of events that seemed so unfair. One day over lunch with Dr. Lester Sumrall, who had spoken at our church, I began to unload my burdens. He listened to me without a word for nearly fifteen minutes while sipping a bowl of soup. When he finished eating, he put down his spoon, looked me in the eye and said, "Young man, perseverance will always outlast persecution." With that he called for the bill and our lunch was over.

We had the fastest-growing church in the city, we were misunderstood and persecuted every step of the way, and we did not know what we had done wrong. But Dr. Sumrall's words rang true. Yes, we were being persecuted, but we were persevering—and surviving. In fact, we were growing. By 1986 we had more than 500 members, people who were hungry for more of God and wanting to learn how to walk in Kingdom principles.

That year, Reinhard Bonnke launched his Fire Conferences in Harare, and most of our congregation got involved to help coordinate the meetings and follow-up. Leaders from all over Africa streamed into Harare and filled the city's brand-new convention center for its very first event. During these exciting meetings, something ignited in my heart that we should be hosting conferences such as this for our own nation. For the next two years I consulted with church leaders in the city trying to persuade them to join together for an annual convention of believers.

In late 1987, God spoke to me, almost in an audible voice, and said, "Pastor the city." I had no idea what this meant and struggled with the idea because I was finding it difficult to pastor my own church, let alone the city. I spent some time fasting and praying in January of the next year, and felt that God instructed me to hold a convention that would take place annually to bless and minister to as many in the body of Christ as could receive. We organized our first event later that year, calling it our Action Conference. Our goal was to motivate the body of Christ to act upon the word of God that they were being taught. Our first guest speakers were Casey and Wendy Treat, who pastor a dynamic ministry in Seattle, Washington, called Christian Faith Center.

They ministered a strong word on "Renewing the Mind," and their participation in the Conference and the great encouragement that they brought to Bonnie and me began a wonderful friendship. In fact, in the next few years Casey and Wendy would be responsible for helping Bonnie with her second album, Created to Praise, by hosting "Bonnie Breakfasts" and raising the money for her to produce her album. We shared the birth of our first children together, and Casey made frequent trips with teams from his church to help strengthen the church here in Zimbabwe.

At that very first Conference, we had no idea how many people would show up, and were surprised when 250 people attended the daytime teachings and workshops, and even more surprised when 500 people came to Harry Margolis Hall for the evening services. There were delegates not just from our church, but also from churches throughout Harare and Zimbabwe, and from all over southern Africa.

The response was astonishing. People told us how encouraged they were, how God had ministered to them during the teachings, and how motivating it was to be together as the body of Christ.

We have held Action Conferences almost every year since then, and they have grown to be one of the major Christian events on the continent of Africa. Nearly 2,000 delegates from all over the world attend the leadership workshops during the day, and as many as 7,000 attend evening sessions. Leaders regularly attend from throughout Africa, Europe, Australia, and the United States—not just as speakers, but also as delegates. We have kept the meetings non-denominational and open to all, and they carry no outward affiliation with any specific church or movement, including ours, in an effort to create a spirit of unity and cooperation.

God has brought some of the most anointed men and women from all over the world to teach at the Conferences: Dr. Lester Sumrall, Dr. Edwin Cole, Dick Mills, Rick Godwin,

Dr. A.R. Bernard, Lafayette Scales, Richard Roberts, Larry Stockstill, Dr. John Stanko, Jeff Perry, Wayne Myers, Phil Pringle, Ray McCauley, Joseph Garlington, Marilyn Hickey, Betty Maltz, Bobby Jean Merck, Alan and Eileen Vincent, David Loveless, Jim and Debbie Cobrae, Bayless Conley, and many others from around the world. We have been blessed by the ministry of great men from the continent of Africa including Joe Imakonda and Bernard Nwaka of Zambia, Mark Kiriuki of Kenya, Enock Sitima from Botswana, and Apostle Gabenga and Dr. Udofia from Nigeria, along with key leaders of the church in Zimbabwe including Ezekiel Guti, Tudor Bismarck, Ngwiza Mkandla, Ricky Decker, James Grey, and Langton Gatsi.

These men and women, and many others, have helped to strengthen the body of Christ in Africa and expose the African church to what God is doing elsewhere in the world. At the Action 98 Conference, we were the first organization in southern Africa to host a live internet broadcast, which featured real-time sound and video feed of the Conference messages. The response was overwhelming, and all available lines were filled for the duration of each of the main sessions. We had thousands of hits from all over the world.

From the first Conference, the Lord has used Bonnie's musical gifts to bless thousands of people—not only by singing and coordinating worship for the events, but also through teaching musicians, artists, and worship leaders who were hungry for good training in the ministry to which God had called them. God took the young woman who gave up a promising music career in the United States, and gave her opportunities to minister to many people—not only at Action Conferences, but in other settings as well. Just a few years after she arrived in Africa, she hosted a praise and worship seminar that attracted 1,000 people from many denominations all over the nation. We ran out of seats, and it was literally standing-room-only. In 1986, Reinhard Bonnke asked Bonnie to coordinate worship at his Fire Conference in Harare. Four years later, she ministered at Harmony '90, an international concert in Johannesburg, South Africa, attended by more than 50,000 people. Pregnant with our third son, Benjamin, Bonnie shared the stage with artists such as the Imperials, the Continentals, and Danibelle Hall. Integrity Music recorded her song "I Bow My Knee" on two Hosanna! Music albums, including Majesty, with worship leader Ron Kenoly. Bonnie has also produced her own worship albums, including Created to Praise, You Mean Everything to Me, and Don't Give Up.

The Lord has also given Bonnie a platform for ministry in secular venues. Each December in the mid-90s, she wrote and produced a full-scale presentation for the nation called "Christmas Foretold," featuring more than 350 cast and crew members, a 120-voice choir, with drama, song, dance, and banners. The pageant was filmed by the Zimbabwe Broadcasting Corporation, and aired on national television, where more than 1.6 million people saw an anointed, professional presentation of the Christmas message.

The Bible says that a man's gifts will make room for him to stand before kings. That applies to women, too, of course. In 1993, Bonnie was invited to sing at the inauguration tea for the Sally Mugabe Foundation (named after the late wife of President Mugabe). Bonnie sang the song she wrote for the Zimbabwe National Anthem competition and received a standing ovation. She also had the privilege of ministering in song to 52 heads of state at the Organization of African Unity Summit. Most of Africa's leaders were present, including Muammar Gaddafi (Libya); Palestinian president Yasser Arafat; Frederick Chiluba (Zambia), Nelson Mandela (South Africa), and more than 200 ambassadors and leaders from all over the world.

Even today people stop us in the streets and recall the power of Bonnie's praise and worship ministry and the great impact it has had on the lives of so many. Her great talent and heart to see others reach their full potential in praise and worship drove her to motivate people to a standard of excellence that had not been seen in Africa.

Unless you see the ultimate, you will be enslaved by the immediate.

As our years in Africa turned into decades, God's hand was on both our ministries—yet we faced a new battle. This time it came in a different form than I had ever experienced before, and it nearly destroyed Bonnie and me, for this time the battle was for our marriage. Although we loved each other deeply, we did not see a great rift developing between us. It was not always evident as we shared so much in common; but because of the magnitude of the ministry, we began to drift apart. There was Bonnie with her creative juices flowing with large-scale productions, driving kids to and from school, making sure homework was done, and still overseeing the ladies ministry and the music department. And there I was busy feeding refugees, preaching on Sundays, founding a Bible school, and trying to build platforms for unity in the nation. Our lives became like the proverbial ships passing in the night. We would see each other, if we were lucky, early in the morning and sometimes late at night, but found ourselves too exhausted, both physically and emotionally, to respond to each other's needs.

The inevitable happened and our marriage hit the rocks. When it did, many who said they were our friends forsook us, and some of the congregation whom we had loved and nurtured could not understand what was happening between us. Bonnie and I found ourselves in the winter of our marriage. In our own darkest hour, when our nation seemed to be in its darkest hour also, God saw fit to provide the opportunity to build our church building. He gave Bonnie and me a wake-up call, and we have diligently studied our lives and our marriage, refocusing our intentions on making the important things the important things. No ministry or ministry opportunity is more important than our marriage covenant and our family. God began working with Bonnie and me to rebuild our marriage and our ministry values. He surrounded us with faithful and loyal partners in ministry as well as good friends, both locally and abroad. Once again, I am amazed at how He takes the foolish things to confound the wise, and the least to do great things. I take great comfort in the fact that when we are weak, we are made strong. He is not a God of condemnation.

Between droughts both natural and spiritual, persecution that I never thought we could endure, and surviving the winter of our marriage, Bonnie and I truly learned to lean on God in all difficulties. I would never have believed that we could go through such hardships in our lives, yet at the same time experience such a sense of destiny.

Perhaps God did not want us to get too comfortable where we were, because He had bigger plans for us. In the midst of intense hardships, unrelenting persecution, and phenomenal growth, God began to speak to us about opening our eyes to a much bigger picture than the one we saw in Harare. In April 1996, we changed the name of our church from Rhema Bible Church to Hear the Word Church, to reflect our broader outreach. We also launched Hear the Word Ministries to encompass all our outreach efforts. Although I was very excited about the rapid growth of our local church, I knew that God did not send me to Africa just to start another city church. In fact, from the moment I had arrived in Africa in 1979, He was continually stretching me and expanding my vision—from teaching at the African Bible College in the capital, to evangelizing in the districts, to pastoring the city of Harare.

Now He was challenging me to pastor not just a city but a region—the five nations of central Africa. He did not even specify which five nations, but I knew He was challenging me to open my eyes to see the harvest field beyond the city gates.

Bonnie and I were married October 24, 1981

Our early days of ministry, 1983

First service at Mt. Pleasant Hall, Harare, Zimbabwe

Fourteen weeks after we started our church, we purchased an office complex that served as headquarters for the next 20 years.

*Unloading our first sound system
in Johannesburg, South Africa, 1982*

With Bonnie, early ministry in rural Zimbabwe

With Bonnie, early ministry in rural Zimbabwe

Bonnie and I with (from left) Paul Grier, Dr. Lester Sumrall, and Lou Montecalvo, who joined us to do relief work and to speak at Action '91

My mentor and friend, Dr. Edwin Louis Cole, at Action '96

Mrs. Parirenyatwa, wife of Zimbabwe's minister of health, opens the orphanage complex at Ivordale Farm, 1998.

Top: Celebration Center concrete and steel super- structure takes shape.

Right: Watching the foundation of Celebration Center being poured, early 1998

Bottom: Our church meets in the shell of Celebration Center, 1999.

The completed structure

The Deuschle Family: (standing) Tommy, Bonnie, Sarah, Tom; (seated) Jonathan, Daniel, and Benjamin

Chapter 5

Renaissance or Reformation?

I f you took a piece of paper and drew a line down the middle, and listed on one side all of Zimbabwe's natural advantages, and on the other side all the disadvantages, you would be amazed at how lopsided your paper would be—with the "advantage" side outweighing the disadvantage side. Zimbabwe is rich in mineral resources, and filled with fertile agricultural land. The per capita gross domestic product (GDP) is twice the average of many other sub-Saharan nations.[4] In fact, compared with other African countries, Zimbabwe is wealthy.

So why is there so much poverty in this country? Why is the unemployment rate nearly 50 percent? Why did inflation rise from 32 percent in 1998 to nearly double that a year later?

In his book *Culture Matters*, Lawrence E. Harrison makes a fascinating comparison of two countries—Ghana and South Korea. Fifty years ago at the end of the Korean War, both countries had nearly the same rock-bottom GDP. Both were Christianized at the same time. So why today does South Korea have the twelfth-largest economy in the world, while Ghana remains in poverty? Could the answer go back to that piece of paper listing advantages and disadvantages? Could the answer be not just in the natural wealth, but also in the need for a cultural and spiritual awakening, as South Korea has experienced?

Long ago, the Lord spoke to me about the issues that Zimbabweans faced on a daily basis, and I felt compelled to address them. In my early years in ministry, He taught me that pat answers and simple maxims weren't enough when people were traumatized by war, drought, devastation, and violence on a daily basis. They needed unchangeable and proven truths that were grounded in the word of God.

Could it be that the answer for our society was to let God's people out of the box they were locked in, and set them loose on every area of society? Jesus taught His disciples to pray, "Your kingdom come...on earth as it is in heaven" (Matthew 6:10 NIV), and He promised to establish an everlasting Kingdom that would never pass away (see Psalm 145:13 and Daniel 7:27). Bonnie and I believed that, if we asked, He would show us exactly how to inaugurate that Kingdom—in our cities, states, and countries.

We began to build dreams, and build people in the process. For example, we started to teach our young people that it was not enough to get a job and work for someone else. They needed to believe God that they could own their own companies. It was not enough to be employees; they could be employers. It was not enough to work for money; they could put money to work for them. It was not enough to get a good education; they needed to become the educators. It was not enough to have the power to vote; they needed to be actively involved in the political process.

The kingdom of God is where reformation takes place, and God began to show us that the church *could* bring reformation to society. We weren't the only ones hearing this word, of course; in a handful of places around the world, a small (and usually misunderstood) group of His people were working to break the church out of the four walls and bring Kingdom principles to business, medicine, education, finance, the arts, and every area of their culture. Not surprisingly, they ran into opposition, just as we did, from those who believed the church had no business in these arenas. We believed the church had no business staying out of them. In fact, the history of Africa proves that only the kingdom of God can bring lasting change in these arenas. There is no hope apart from it.

Renaissance Cannot Happen Without Reformation

We have seen God raise up a new generation of leaders in all arenas of society who have learned to stand up for righteousness and a righteous Lord, to defend their natural and spiritual families against all adversaries. These men and women of integrity made decisions to live by biblical standards, and God has placed them in strategic positions where they could make a difference in their countries and cultures. They have been instrumental in bringing true reformation not only to the church, but to the institutions of society as well.

When apartheid was dismantled in South Africa, which was the last nation on the continent to be under the yoke of colonialism, there was a great cry from now President Thabo Mbeki for an "African renaissance." Although there needs to be an enlightenment (and this could very well be the season when Africa begins to shine), *renaissance cannot happen without reformation*—a reformation of the very principles upon which all of society is based, in every nation. The role of the church and gospel of Jesus Christ is to bring the much-needed message that can effect this reformation in the nations.

Centuries ago, Martin Luther brought reformation to the church, and the church, in turn, changed the society around it, producing a dynamic economic development that has affected Europe and North America to this day. Mariano Grondona writes,

> It was more than a Protestant reformation; it was a "Protestant cultural revolution [that] changed the map of Europe by affecting all the nations that had been ranked as second-rank nations—Holland, Switzerland, Great Britain, Scandinavian countries, Prussia and the former British colonies of North America. Economic development followed the cultural awakening in the form of the Industrial Revolution and with it came power, wealth and prestige to a new group of leaders."[5]

Note that it was not the renaissance of Italy, the Vatican, or France that ushered in the change; it was a reformation based solidly on Kingdom principles.

Before we see another renaissance, we need another reformation. Just as Babylon was shaken by the influence of Daniel, Shadrach, Meshach, and Abednego; just as the character of England was changed because of the preaching of John and Charles Wesley; and just as America was impacted by the spiritual awakenings of the eighteenth and nineteenth centuries, it is time for the church in Africa to clearly spell out the principles of reformation for Africa. All of the "isms" from colonialism to communism have been tried and have proved wanting on the African continent. Now the deeply spiritual African people are crying out for substance and spiritual reality. This is something that religion cannot offer, because religion—no matter what brand—is simply man's attempt to reach God.

Today there is an awakening in the hearts of Africans of all nations, creeds, genders, tribes, and denominations who want to look past their differences and focus on a common denominator, principles that are set forth clearly in the word of God that will bring genuine reformation. These principles are the only hope for dismantling the deep-seated corruption, jealousy, intimidation, genocide, ethnic cleansings, authoritarianism, tribal factionalism, and many of the other "isms" that have ravaged and beset Africa. Until they are dismantled, we will not see this great "African renaissance" take place.

To do this, it will take a new breed of believers willing to live by conviction, not preference; by principle, not culture. Through their actions they will challenge the status quo, and through righteous dissent overthrow corruption, greed, and evil. For a nation to progress, there are certain elements that must be reflected in its culture. Until these elements are part of the fabric of the society, that society will not be in a position to develop. Kingdom-generated reformation must include these principles:

Principle one: The kingdom of God is based on transparency and trust. Until this is the basis of our dealings with each other, we will never see reformation. The very nature of African tribalism is not to trust. Tribalism engenders suspicion fostered by domination and control shrouded in fear.

To trust the individual, to have faith in the individual is one of the elements of a value system that favors development. In contrast mistrust of the individual, reflected in oversight and control, is typical of societies that resist development. Implicit in the trusting society is the willingness to accept the risk that the individual will make choices contrary to the desires of government. If this risk is not accepted and the in-

dividual is subjected to a network of controls, the society loses the essential engine of economic development, namely, the aspiration of each of us to live and
think as we wish, to be who we are, to transform
ourselves into unique beings. Where there are no individuals, only "peoples" and "masses," development
does not occur. What takes place instead is either
obedience or uprising.[6]

Trust inherently relates to a firm belief in the reliability,
truth, or strength of a person or thing. It is the state of being
relied upon. The basis of the kingdom of God is not only
that God can be relied upon, but also that those who are His
representatives on earth can be relied upon. The foundation
of this trust is that God speaks the truth and can be relied
upon, and that men who are governed by the principles of
God's Kingdom will do likewise. On this foundation, we can
transform not only culture, but also nations.

**Principle two: The kingdom of God exhibits a value for
life.** It is often said of Africa that life is cheap there. Life expectancy is less than 60 years in 28 countries, and below 50
years in 18 countries. In Zimbabwe, life expectancy is just
38 years for men, and less than 36 for women. Poverty, of
course, is staggering across the continent. The World Bank
reports that half of the 600 million people in sub-Saharan
Africa live in poverty. In at least 13 countries, at least half
the adult population is illiterate. In many countries, ten percent of children die before the age of five. Yet the population
growth rate in sub-Saharan Africa is nearly three percent
annually, almost four times the rate found in high-income
countries. And of course the enormity of the AIDS pandemic is astonishing; Zimbabwe has the highest rate of infection in the world.

What one judges as being valuable or important in life is

based on the principles and standards one chooses to uphold. The lower the principle, the lower the value. If man is viewed as being formed by God and valued by God, and life is sacred, then his worth and desirability increase. However, if the converse is true, man simply becomes a commodity, a piece on the chess board, willing to be traded for any other piece of relative rank or importance according to whatever set of rules happen to be in place. Without Kingdom standards set in place, values simply revert to the lowest common denominator, and man begins to operate by the law of the jungle—the law of survival of the fittest.

Principle three: The kingdom of God is established on an attitude of faith toward wealth. A Kingdom culture believes that wealth consists of what does not yet exist. This is a scriptural principle based on Romans 4:17: "God who gives life to the dead and calls things that are not as though they were" (NIV). Non-progressive cultures, on the other hand, believe that wealth consists of what exists. That is why in the developing world there is so much emphasis placed on land and what derives from it, while in the developed world wealth derives from new innovations and investing in the future.

This principle, or the lack of it, also affects the attitude toward competition. The kingdom of God promotes healthy competition, which is essential for everything from politics to free enterprise. A Kingdom mentality looks not at what already is in the marketplace with a jealous eye to possess, but rather at what can be built in the future to increase market share and bring with it benefits such as wealth creation, jobs, and increased prosperity. The word of God says, "With me are riches and honor, enduring wealth and prosperity...bestowing wealth on those who love me and making their treasuries full" (Proverbs 8:18, 21 NIV). When competition is viewed negatively, the result is jealousy and all kinds of utopian dreams, bolstered by words such as loyalty, cooperatives, monopolies, cartels, and the like; the only place that real competition is allowed is in sports.

Principle four: The kingdom of God leaves an inheritance for future generations. The psalmist said that God's people "store up wealth for their children" (Psalm 17:14 NIV). King Solomon said, "A good man leaves an inheritance for his children's children" (Proverbs 13:22 NIV).

As citizens of God's Kingdom, our goal should be to leave an inheritance for our children's children—to pass on wealth to the next generation so that they can build on what previous generations have already accomplished. Traditional African culture, on the other hand, emphasizes the present and meeting the immediate needs of those alive now. In part, this is a response to poverty and urgent needs, but it is also a result of practices that surround ancestral worship, which always takes from the younger to give to the older. Many of these practices have a financial element that benefits not a future generation but the older generation.

This is contrary to biblical principles, which admonish one generation to leave an inheritance for the next (except in the case of widows and orphans, who are to be cared for). Basic to the principle of leaving an inheritance for future generations is the principle of sowing and reaping, which God demonstrates through His Word. Seedtime and harvest will never fail as long as the earth remains. To have a harvest, we must sow seed into the ground. To expect a harvest with no seed in the ground is an attempt to operate God's principle illegally. We cannot leave a harvest for future generations if we do not plant seeds for it in this generation.

Everything we do at Hear the Word Church and Ministries is according to a pattern that others can follow. We record everything in order to leave an inheritance for the next generation. All our messages are taped, and all our business meetings are in writing so that our sons and daughters can see our mistakes as well as our victories. They can look back and say, "Yes, they erred, but this is what they were thinking." This becomes a learning process for the next generation.

Sadly, so many visions die with the current generation. I may be founder and senior pastor of the church, and leader of the ministry, but I do not believe in building a vision around myself; it has to be a generational vision, for my children's children and my spiritual children. We will not know if we are a success until our great-grandchildren's generation. If what we have built lasts until then, it will be successful.

Principle five: The kingdom of God teaches the value of a proper relationship to authority. We are constantly moving between being *in authority* and being *under authority* in our relationships with people, whether they be friendships, work relationships, or public or private office. The degree to which we manage these relationships is the degree to which we have success in life.

God Himself is directly involved with various institutions of authority in the world. The first institution of authority is the individual. Individuals who take responsibility for governing themselves under the rulership of God (self-control) can change (or reform) the second institution of authority— families. Families who, in turn, operate under righteous authority change their churches, and churches change nations, which must also be under righteous authority.

When authority drifts toward a dictator and away from the rule of law, people learn to adapt themselves to the arbitrary whims of those in power. This wreaks devastation both in the psyche and structure of society and gives way to corruption. When the pendulum swings back to the rule of law, however, law-abiding citizens willingly uphold that law. When a nation or a people allow their laws to rule them, rather than the personality of the chiefs, kings, or other rulers, it is for the betterment of the society. Self-government is always better than institutional government. Both are necessary but nations advance more rapidly according to the degree of self-governance. Believers who studiously attempt to walk according to God's law understand how to be in authority and under authority in any given situation in life. These believers become great citizens. In fact, they become what the Bible describes as salt and light to a tasteless and dark world.

Principle six: The kingdom of God exhibits intentionality—intentionally making room for people of all "nations, tribes, and languages." In John's account in the book of Revelation of his vision of heaven, he described seeing "a great multitude that no one could count, from every nation, tribe, people and language, standing before the throne and in front of the Lamb" (Revelation 7:9 NIV). If the kingdom of God looks like that in heaven, shouldn't our churches look like that on earth? Such churches do not happen by accident; they are built as we intentionally and deliberately open our arms, hearts, and doors to people of all nations, tribes, and languages.

This is not easy, particularly in a country such as Zimbabwe that has been torn apart by racial hatred, but that was our vision from the beginning. In the early days, we attracted many white faces, I assume because they were comforted by the fact that as the senior pastor I was white—but that is not an accurate picture of Zimbabwe. The reality is that Zimbabwe and Africa are more than 99 percent black. We felt our church had to be more reflective of the population, rather than drawing from only a small segment.

As Joseph Garlington of Reconciliation Ministries says, "In a divided society, only the church can model unity." That is why we believed it was imperative that we build and model a multicultural church. At first it was difficult to attract black African leaders and members—I'm sure for a number of good reasons. Many of the white missionaries and white church leaders had either taken on the trappings of colonialism or created structures that made church members and leaders dependent on outside help. We began to address this by intentionally creating opportunities that would attract strong leaders. We started working with young black leaders who embraced the message of the kingdom of God, and also reached out to the other communities in Zimbabwe's multicultural society— colored,[7] Indian, and the many tribes, ethnic groups, and nationalities.

We knew that if we were to model true reconciliation, we not only had to worship together, but also live the gospel together. The story of Jacob and his father, Laban, became the pattern from which we developed these principles of reconciliation in our congregation (see Genesis chapter 30). Jacob placed speckled branches in front of the eyes of goats and sheep; genetically these animals should never have been able to produce speckled goats and sheep, but because of what they saw at the watering holes and pastures, the Bible indicates very strongly that was how they reproduced.

With this in mind we developed a rule that whenever we ministered, we would do so with a "speckled branch." Every time there was public ministry, we intentionally featured both black and white, colored, Indian, and any other nationality we could, and we presented them before the eyes of the congregation. It has been a blessing to see this principle take hold and continue to foster a cross-cultural mix in our church membership, and the church has become a congregation representing all nations, all ethnic groups, and all tribes coming together in unity.

Sadly, once the church was more than 50 percent black African in its membership, many of the white African members began to feel uncomfortable. We lost people who could not see the vision or embrace it, either because it was too large or too frightening, or because they were faced with their own prejudices and fears—the age-old battle of class and racial prejudice.

During the past 30 years, there has been a mass exodus of Europeans from Rhodesia and now Zimbabwe, something known as "white flight." In the early days of the church, this had a negative affect not only on me as a leader, but also on our congregation, because each year hundreds of people would emigrate—often with little or no warning. Over the past 20 years, I estimate more than 5,000 of our church members emigrated. Many of them would speak negatively about the country, their church, and their lives in Zimbabwe, in order to justify their departure. These negative words, attitudes, and actions sent tidal waves across the congregation, and each year I felt compelled to speak on topics such as building vision, national pride, honoring heroes, the blessing of faithfulness, and leaving an inheritance for future generations.

Yet we persevere because we know that in a divided society such as the one we live in, only the church can model unity. Our focus continues to be building and modeling a multicultural church.

Principle seven: The kingdom of God gives man dominion over the earth. This is the biblical worldview, based on Genesis when God told Adam and Eve that they had dominion over all creation. As long as they obeyed Him, dominion was theirs (see Hebrews 2:8). When they fell, however, they lost the glory and image of God, and lost dominion over Creation. Satan took the throne vacated by Adam and Eve, and exercised his dominion over the earth, and death filled the world (see Hebrews 2:14-15).

All the generations following Adam and Eve have inherited their fallen nature, and all have come under the power and dominion of Satan. God, however, provided salvation through Jesus Christ and the cross of Calvary. Jesus came into the world to rescue mankind from Satan's power. Jesus gave His life as a ransom to buy us back, destroy the works of Satan in our lives, and return dominion to mankind.

Once again we have dominion over the earth through Christ, with the God-ordained power to rule, subdue, and change the earth. Unfortunately, much religion and witchcraft paint the picture of a world filled with irresistible forces that have the power to overwhelm the individual. Whether these forces are called God, gods, the devil, scientific socialism, capitalism, Marxism, or Zionism, our worldview determines how we live. Many in Africa are still bound by a fear of witchcraft. So many African people are waiting for life to happen to them, but God designed man to be the protagonist and make life happen.

Only the kingdom of God can bring true reformation to a society. Islam and other religions have tried, and of course have failed, but sadly traditional Christianity has failed, too, particularly in Africa. The church must take a hard look at itself because, until now, it has not truly affected African ancestral beliefs nor changed the basic cultural understanding of the contemporary societies on the continent. It is difficult to question a culture, but until we can change some key elements of the African culture, we will be forced to live according to the old proverb, "Attempting the same things, expecting to get different results."

The kingdom of God is the answer for every problem on earth, whether in Africa, the United States, or elsewhere.

The answer for Africa is not to look to capitalism, free enterprise, or the so-called developed nations. If Africans would look with all their heart to the word of God, they would find that what God promises is far better than the materialism of the West or the asceticism of the East. Africa does not have to remain a culture bankrupt by witchcraft, but we can develop a culture built on respect for human life with all of the virtues and values set forth in the Scriptures. Then Isaiah chapter 60 will become a living reality for the people who for too many years have been written off as the "Dark Continent."

> Arise, shine, for your light has come,
> And the glory of the Lord rises upon you.
> See, darkness covers the earth
> And thick darkness is over the peoples,
> But the Lord rises upon you
> And his glory appears over you.
> Nations will come to your light,
> And kings to the brightness of your dawn.
> Lift up your eyes and look about you:
> All assemble and come to you;
> Your sons come from afar,
> And your daughters are carried on the arm.
> Then you will look and be radiant,
> Your heart will throb and swell with joy;
> The wealth on the seas will be brought to you,
> To you the riches of the nations will come.
> Herds of camels will cover your land,
> Young camels of Midian and Ephah.
> And all from Sheba will come,
> Bearing gold and incense
> And proclaiming the praise of the Lord.
> All Kedar's flocks will be gathered to you,

The rams of Nebaioth will serve you;
They will be accepted as offerings on my altar,
And I will adorn my glorious temple (Isaiah 60:1-7 NIV).

CHAPTER 6

21st-Century Reformation

When I first started pastoring, it did not take me long to learn that I did not have the answers for the ills of society. In fact, no pastor does. To some extent we have glorified pastors so that they are expected to be experts on almost every subject, as if they are the only ones who can hear from God. We have made them mega-leaders who speak and the world stops to listen (at least the church world).

I remember that first church meeting in our home back in 1982 when Bonnie led worship, I preached, and we were both exhausted by the time our enormous congregation of six went home. God, of course, has a much better plan (or no pastor would ever hold a second church meeting), which He clearly sets forth in Ephesians 4:11-12: "He [God]...gave some to be apostles, some to be prophets, some to be evangelists, and some to be pastors and teachers, to prepare God's people for works of service, so that the body of Christ may be built up" (NIV).

Our job as pastors, evangelists, apostles, prophets, and teachers is to "prepare God's people for works of service," or as another version puts it, "for the work of the ministry" (NKJ). You could also call it "building people and building dreams." We are heads of families that are called churches, and our role is to disciple and train our sons and daughters so that they can they become great in whatever sphere they are in. We give them instruction and say, "This is what the Kingdom looks like. Now go and make a difference."

It is my firm belief that the next wave of leadership in the church will not be only clerical, but will include workers and leaders from every arena of society. Men and women will be raised up to serve in the areas God has gifted them for the extension of the kingdom of God on earth in every facet of life—because He is concerned with all of life, not just church life.

I did not arrive in Africa with this understanding, of course, nor did I have the benefit of reading the previous chapter in this book when I got here—but that might have been a good thing. Because we did not have any model to follow, we were able to pioneer our own way and think creatively. There was a lot of trial and error, making mistakes, learning from what we had done wrong, and realizing what God was trying to do in us and through us. Now, with the benefit of 20/20 hindsight, I can look at the past two decades and see what God has been up to—the areas of our society where He has been strategically at work to bring reformation. Here is some of what we have done to reform our society, what we plan to do in the future, and the scriptural principles that motivate us.

Reformation in the Business Arena

Until we have a revival in the business community, we will not see a spiritual revival. That may seem like a strange statement, but I believe it to be true. We have had a wonderful era of evangelism, but not of discipleship. To be frank, it seems as if everyone in Africa has raised their hands a dozen times at altar calls and mass crusades. Next week the same one million will raise their hands again, this time at someone else's crusade. Look closely and watch them worship, and you will see they know what they are doing because they have been in church for years. If, in fact, there has been such a revival in country after country on the continent, why don't we see the results throughout the rest of society? Why hasn't the revival inside the church spilled over into the community? The answer is because *we are doing a great job evangelizing, but not discipling*. Without an economic revival based on biblical principles, we can say goodbye to Africa. When people are starving to death, they need something more. James wrote:

> *What good is it, my brothers, if a man claims to have faith but has no deeds? Can such faith save him? Suppose a brother or sister is without clothes and daily food. If one of you says to him, "Go, I wish you well; keep warm and well fed," but does nothing about his physical needs, what good is it? In the same way, faith by itself, if it is not accompanied by action, is dead* (James 2:14-17 NIV).

The need for an economic revival based on biblical principles is one of the reasons our church launched an organization called Victory Business Forum (VBF)—to help raise up, disciple, and train business people and professionals to carry out the mandate of bringing God's Kingdom to the earth. We created VBF to instill this understanding and vision in as many business leaders as possible and to help them express and develop their God-given gifts and talents. VBF empowers them to go from "vision to victory" (the VBF mandate) by realizing that the power to gain wealth, along with individual gifts, talents, and resources, is God's enabling blessing in order to establish His Kingdom on earth.

VBF is comprised of men and women who are called to serve God not in the traditional sense of preaching, teaching, or evangelism, but as business people who know that their work is their ministry. The Bible says that God "has made us kings and priests unto God" (Revelation 1:6 NIV). God is raising up a new breed of business and professional people who are passionate about His Kingdom. VBF gives them an opportunity to develop their gifts and help them rediscover their destiny by stepping into the plan that God has for their lives. The goal is to produce leaders who are servants, disciples, and mentors who in turn will affect their own personal circle of friends and business partners. As a result, we are producing leaders who walk in prosperity, and know they are blessed so that they, in turn, can be a blessing to the nations.

Victory Business Forum members are committed to these core values:

1. **Obedience**: Honoring God in paying the tithe and giving freewill offerings to their local church.

2. **Commitment**: Fulfilling the calling on our lives by surrendering our careers and resources to the Lord to advance His Kingdom.

3. **Integrity**: Living biblical standards in the practice of all business and life affairs, and being a light that reflects the character of Jesus Christ to the world.

4. **Submission**: Walking under the authority of a local pastor and being accountable through discipleship to the leadership of a local church.

5. **Values**: Standing up for righteousness and for our Lord Jesus Christ, defending our natural and spiritual family against all adversaries.

Members meet regularly for training and leadership development, seminars, workshops, and ministry events. They are mentored by committed leaders who have not only demonstrated success, but want to disciple others to do the same and make them part of a winning team. In every activity, VBF members learn Kingdom principles coupled with strategic advice and wise counsel to help them develop a sound business and life strategy for today's challenging world. With the goal of "vision to victory," we hammer into the minds of young business people the need to have vision for more than the church in order to develop resources and people who can fund Kingdom projects.

Sue Mbaya, one of our church members who is actively involved on the board of VBF, always knew that God wanted to use her beyond her immediate circle of influence, but never confessed it to anyone for fear of being thought too presumptuous. Instead she went through the motions of appearing satisfied with a successful position as a business consultant, even thought her success came at the expense of her family life. Deep inside she knew something was missing.

"In 1997, the Lord challenged me to 'seek first His Kingdom,'" Sue says, and she dropped out of the business world to devote herself to the needs of her family. "I gave up power, control, financial security, and the luxury of corporate life out of obedience to God. In the face of disapproval from my colleagues, I strove to establish a family life that was based on biblical principles."

In return, God sovereignly established her in a new career as the only female research consultant in the agricultural sector in southern Africa. Today she is in a strategic position to influence the thinking of non-governmental organizations that are developing policy on land issues—a key concern in many African countries today. "In addition, I enjoy modeling the fruits of a life that is submitted to

Christ," she says. "The most significant lesson I have had to learn was that of God's immeasurable desire to bless me financially through my giving. Through the ministry of anointed men and women of God, I have learned to put into practice the biblical principles relating to sowing and reaping, faithful tithing, the power of sowing into the life of a man of God, and the role of a business person in providing for the vision of the man of God. It is with this desire in my heart that I work toward establishing VBF as a place of servanthood and a place of prosperity."

Vincent Tendayi is another church member and VBF board member who has seen God do extraordinary things through his work in the business sector—in spite of the fact that he works in the building industry in Zimbabwe, which suffered greatly during the droughts of past years.

"1998 was a very difficult year for my company," Vincent explains. "The building industry was experiencing a downturn in business, and 1999 promised to be a more difficult year."

I met with Vincent, shared with him my vision for a new church building, and talked about how his company could help. "I thought God had heard our prayers," Vincent remembers, "and [that He had] thrown out a lifeline with this big contract for supplying and fixing all the aluminum works and suspended ceilings for the church building project. It was the biggest project I tendered for that year besides the New Reserve Bank of Zimbabwe project."

Vincent could have stopped there, but he made a bold decision to provide the materials at cost—in the midst of a sliding economy and with little resources of his own. "I did not have other supporting contracts to pay for the labor or running costs," he says. In fact, Vincent was facing bankruptcy, but he saw the opportunity to sow seed "on time, in the right season," he says. "In faith I held fast to God's

Word: 'I can do everything through him who gives me strength' (Philippians 4:13 NIV). My life and business have been founded on the principle of being faithful to uphold the vision of building God's house for future generations."

God was faithful and has blessed Vincent with good clients and other business so that he has never gone without. "I met all the costs on time," he says, "and the recognition [that] my company has gained in the industry is phenomenal. I attribute the success of my company to God."

Reformation in the Medical Arena

Pick every negative word you can think of, and you have a good description of the medical situation in Zimbabwe. Consider these frightening statistics

1. Life expectancy is just 38 years for men, and less than 36 years for women.[8]

2. Zimbabwe has the world's highest rate of HIV/AIDS infection.[9]

3. Officially, 30 percent of the population has the disease, although the United Nations says as many as 50 percent may be dying from it.

4. Nearly one million children in Zimbabwe have lost both parents to AIDS and are now orphans—almost ten percent of the population.

Add to these staggering figures an antiquated medical model dating from approximately 1950, and you have a medical crisis of staggering proportions. On top of this, Zimbabweans believe it is culturally correct to be loyal to their own doctor, no matter how far away he is or even if his specialty is different from the one they require.

Our goal is to help reform the medical situation in Zimbabwe, and then the rest of Africa, and bring it to a first-world status. We are working in a number of innovative areas, including partnering with an internationally known medical organization to turn our old building into a state-of-the-art family health practice and eventually to build a 209-bed world-class hospital next to our new Hear the Word Ministries complex.

The facility will offer service at very high standards, which people will be able to access via an innovative payment method that addresses some of the shortcomings of current medical funding and insurance. They will have access to good private healthcare through a mechanism that allows them to pool resources as families or groups. It will increase their options for treatment, thereby freeing them from feeling obligated to visit their own doctor. This may sound unusual to the western mind, but in the African culture this will be nothing short of revolutionary.

The entire program will be truly unique because although the facility will be jointly owned by the church and a company of one of our members (see Dr. Matthew Wazara's testimony in the next chapter), it will be run as a profitable business, and the church will have the option of offering free services from their portion of the profits. The church becomes a business partner and earns a profit, which it uses to fund the ministry work. This will greatly lessen our dependence on donors, because the church will become more self-sufficient.

Reformation in the medical arena by necessity must come with reformation in the education arena. As such, we are working to help provide:

1. Medical education (post-graduate and nursing)
2. Patient education (creating a population of patients who participate in their own care by understanding their conditions and need)
3. Working with and learning from other health-care leaders around the world.

And since God has given us a vision to reach the five nations of central Africa, we also organize medical missions to visit these countries and provide much-needed medical assistance. Medical professionals and caregivers from our church have partnered with medical teams from around the world to provide care on the field, and to create blueprints for enhancing and reforming existing medical systems that are outdated and ineffective.

Reformation in the Education Arena

Education is a sticky subject in Zimbabwe because it is virtually sacred. Rhodesia was built to be a utopian society for white people, and education was high on the list of priorities. In fact, Cecil J. Rhodes, who founded Rhodesia, also established the renowned Rhodes scholar program.

Even after Rhodesia was dissolved and Zimbabwe was created, that reverence for education never faltered, and education in a sense continues to be worshiped here. The top "who's who" lists in the world include many Zimbabweans, and the country's literacy rate is very high; 85 percent of men and women over the age of 15 can read and write.[10] Excellent education is provided here, and the education system is good, unlike the rest of Africa. There are 40,000 students enrolled in universities and colleges.

Half of Zimbabwe's population is under the age of 15, so a good education system is critical, but success has come at a huge premium, because when we worship something other than God, it turns around and bites us—and that is exactly what has happened in Zimbabwe. Because education is an idol, those in charge resist any change. The education structure is badly in need of change, with students being assessed solely on the basis of O and A level exam results. There is little emphasis on vocational training and even less on music and the arts. The system becomes more and more en-

trenched in academics and teaching, while there is very
little emphasis on training. Truly knowledge is power in
Zimbabwe, but those who know "how" are always going to
be at the mercy of those who know "why."

That is why HTWM has started our own schools—a
nursery school, a day-care facility, a Bible school, and an
ACE learning center, which is an educational curriculum
that teaches students to take responsibility for their own education and presents information with a biblical worldview.

These schools are successful, but in themselves they will
not reform the education arena of the country; they are just
setting up another system. To truly bring needed reform
based on Kingdom principles, we have begun seminars to as-
sist high school graduates and university students to interface with successful Christian business leaders and learn the
values and principles that have guided their careers to success. We have created a forum that meets annually called
"Work-place," which addresses issues of integrity, work
ethic, dressing for success, personal hygiene, and biblical
ethics for the marketplace. To date, hundreds of men and
women have applied the lessons they learned at Work-place,
and become more marketable as well as more focused on
the vision and future their lives hold. Not only does this
have a profound effect upon future leaders, but it also brings
a sense of responsibility and accountability to current
leaders from different sectors of society who share with students about how to apply Christian values in the marketplace.

We have also taken teams of young people to the United
States, where they were hosted in major cities by community leaders, small business owners, and captains of industry. One group of students met with the manager of
Madison Square Gardens in New York; with a McDonald's
franchise owner in Pittsburgh who told them about fran-

chise opportunities; with a pastor and businessmen in Dallas, who talked about the relationship between the kingdom of God and business, and with a very successful entrepreneur on the West coast who told them his strong conviction that God is the one who gives us the ability to get wealth. "What we do with wealth when we get it," he said, "is serve God, our communities, and our families." Needless to say, when these young people returned home, they not only became more involved in their churches, but they also had a vision for changing their communities in the same way they ran their businesses. They also wanted to obtain more education—not because they saw education as their source, but because they saw how God could use them when they were properly trained and educated.

For many years, we have operated a Bible school, which we launched in 1984 with 35 students from Zimbabwe and other countries. Over the years, the school has grown to an annual enrollment of 300 students. Today, Hear the Word Ministries Training Center is fully accredited and offers students a four-year bachelor of arts degree in theology and biblical studies as well as supervised post-graduate studies for masters and doctoral programs. To date, approximately 2,500 students have graduated from all over Africa, taking the lessons learned into their homes, schools, and businesses.

Reformation in the Financial Arena

When God first told me, "You will impact the five nations of central Africa," as a young missionary, I assumed I would pastor a nice church and maybe go on television. But I soon realized that would not impact a nation, much less five nations. Dramatically changing the rate of poverty would impact a nation—especially a country such as Zimbabwe where 60 percent of the people live below the poverty line. Reversing the horrific inflation rate would impact a nation—especially Zimbabwe where the current inflation rate is about 116 percent a year. Lowering the unemployment rate would impact a nation—especially Zimbabwe where the unemployment rate is nearly 70 percent. That was the kind of impact I wanted to make, and I still do. As we began to look at reformation of the financial arena, for example, our first step was to inspire our business people to make an impact, and to use the laws of God and the principles of prosperity (as opposed to the American gospel of materialism) to teach the others, raise them up, and help them to take responsibility for the ethics and integrity of the financial institutions in the nation.

Banks, businesses, and universities spend millions of dollars and a tremendous amount of time and effort trying to teach people ethics and integrity. Unfortunately these virtues can neither be legislated nor taught. They come only from a changed life, the fear of God, and a revelation of who He is. The Bible says, "The fear of the Lord is the beginning of knowledge" (Proverbs 1:7 NIV) and "By the fear of the Lord one departs from evil" (Proverbs 16:6 NKJ). In a nation riddled with corruption and greed, biblical reformation is the only answer.

That is the kind of vision and impact it is going to take to bring reformation to the financial world. Our church members include no less than five CEOs and senior managers from the banking world—what an opportunity to engender God-centered ethics into the financial arena! One of them is Nigel Chanakira, founder of the largest investment bank in Zimbabwe. He heads Kingdom Financial Holdings Limited, which is among the top five companies quoted on the Zimbabwe Stock Exchange. Just 36 years old, he has given millions of dollars to fund our outreach projects. He is the "Bill Gates" of Zimbabwe. His goal is to make a billion dollars, and he will tell you that he caught the vision sitting in church.

In 2001, Nigel was nominated as Zimbabwe's manager of the year and was honored as one of the world's 100 future leaders at the Global World Economic Forum held in Davos, Switzerland. Since he caught the vision for reforming his society, he has changed his focus in life to serving his community and improving the state of the world in which he lives and works.

"My principles and values emanate from the word of God, which is my reference manual," Nigel says. "I am learning all the time how doing business God's way is a sure recipe for success—despite adversity, trials, and tribulations that come from running a business in Zimbabwe. There is an inherent connection between expanding Kingdom Financial Holdings and the vision of my church to advance the Kingdom."

Reformation in the Social Arena

In 1983, when I had been in Africa just a few years, someone took me to a local bus stop that was crowded with 200 of the most emaciated and dejected people I had ever seen. Two of them in particular stood out to me, and I can still see them as clearly today as I could then: a mother holding a nearly lifeless baby in her arms. The mother, who was totally naked, was nothing but skin and bones, and so was her baby. The poor child attempted to suck on a piece of skin that was her mother's breast. I walked over to them, and they looked up at me with empty eyes, and I thought, "God, what am I going to do here?"

It broke my heart—and this scene of 200 people was just the tip of the iceberg. These were refugees from Mozambique who had managed to survive a grueling trip across the border into Zimbabwe. Southern Africa had been experiencing severe drought for four years. Mozambique, which is to the east of Zimbabwe, was in the midst of war, and there was no food and little water. People were starving to death, thousands had already died, and entire communities were wiped out. Those who could make it across the border fled to Zimbabwe in search of food and water, and a staggering 150,000 refugees swelled the population of Zimbabwe, but unfortunately conditions here were no better. We too were suffering from the same drought (as was South Africa), and we were still recovering from our own civil war.

The situation nearly overwhelmed me, but I knew I had to do something. Our church was barely a year old, and we had perhaps 200 people. What could such a small group of people do in the face of such tragedy? Bonnie and I asked our members for help, and they responded with enough money to buy an old beat-up ten-ton Bedford truck. We collected seven tons of mealie meal (the staple food of the local diet, made from ground maize), along with some clothing and basic goods. It took us two weeks to collect everything, and we went out on our first relief trip.

By the time we arrived at the bus stop, the number of refugees had swollen from 200 to 2,000. We tried to systematically distribute our gifts, but the people were desperate. They mobbed the truck, and all we could do was grab the keys and literally run for our lives. Three hours later, we were watching desperate people fighting and beating each other for a cup of food. Children were crushed as people fought over the clothing and food we had brought.

We went back to Harare brokenhearted and discouraged. The need was unbelievable, and I knew we had to do something—but it was obvious what we had done was not the answer. For days I wept and felt overwhelmed by the situation.

A few nights later, I got a phone call in the middle of the night. The enthusiastic voice at the other end introduced himself as Ben Kinchlow from the 700 Club and Operation Blessing. I thought it was a joke, put the phone under the pillow, and started laughing to Bonnie that someone was playing a joke on me. I did not know Ben Kinchlow, and I was sure that he did not know me.

But it really was Ben. He knew about the desperate situation with the Mozambican refugees, and somehow had gotten my name. "I understand you're taking care of the refugees," he continued. "Can you use a large amount of rice? We'd like to ship it to you."

Ben offered us a whopping 160 tons of rice. Overnight I became the largest importer of rice in the country. It never failed to astound me how God can take the foolish things of the world and confound the wise, and take the simple and work His plan.

One of the members of my church was a buyer for the Grain Marketing Board of Zimbabwe and negotiated a deal so the Board traded us three bags of mealie meal for each bag of rice. Now we were the largest food relief organization in the country. .

Not being administrators, we stumbled along trying to do the best we could to meet the needs of the refugees. As immediate needs for food and water were met, we shifted to clothing relief, and clothed tens of thousands of refugees. We had a very good relationship with the government, so when they started refugee camps on the border, they allowed our people to live there also. In fact, we were the only organization given that privilege. The people we placed there were evangelists, and they led 65,000 people to Jesus. We started churches in the camps, and the number of church members grew to 38,000. We not only fed and clothed them, but we trained and discipled them in

Kingdom principles to prepare them for the day when they would go back to Mozambique. Those people were all eventually repatriated, and the first thing they did when they got home was start churches. We now have more than 150 churches in Mozambique—all birthed out of our work in those camps. We have partnered with Good News Ministries in Colorado Springs who have built 60 church buildings for them, and we meet with the church leaders in Mozambique on a regular basis for ongoing leadership training.

The drought in Mozambique did not stop at the border, of course, and while we were helping the refugees, our own citizens in Zimbabwe were experiencing the same horrible conditions. In fact, it was the worst drought in the country's history, and as a result, the economic situation deteriorated and prices skyrocketed from month to month. The Lord was so faithful to provide for us and through us in dramatic and miraculous ways, and we felt as if we were living in the book of Acts. People stopped our Compassion Ministries truck in the middle of the bush asking for Jesus. Seven hundred people were born again each month in the refugee camps and among the street people in Harare. There was a real move of God during that time, and people were searching for the Lord as never before.

Of course, the enemy of souls did not let up during this time. Right in the middle of our massive food relief program, a very prominent evangelist from the United States came to Zimbabwe hoping to get into the camps. We were the only group allowed in, so he came to us and asked if we would help him get in and do a TV special—and in exchange, he would channel all his relief help through us.

It turned out to be one of the most successful specials in the history of his ministry. The photographers could not have made the situation look any worse. They opened with a shot of a lavish American dining room table, covered with an abundant Thanksgiving dinner. Then the camera panned to this evangelist who was crying, kneeling in the mud of a refugee camp, and holding a baby covered with flies and feces. He looked right at the camera and said, "While we are spending our time in America like this [referring to the lavish Thanksgiving spread], this is how people are spending it in Zimbabwe."

This man was one of my heroes of the faith—yet he offered all my staff American-level salaries if they would come to work for his organization. He added many incentives that a ministry based in Africa, like ours, could never afford. Sad to say, nearly all of the men and women who had been working for us left us to join his ministry, including my very best friend, whom I thought would work with me forever.

I don't blame anyone for taking the opportunity, although at the time the level of deceit and treachery was nearly unbearable. I knew there was a lesson I had to learn in this, and although at the time, I struggled to see what it might be, today I thank God for once again working on my own character. Eventually this venerated minister fell from ministry, and God showed me how He had protected us because we had not been allowed to align ourselves with his organization. Amazingly his ministry had to sell one of the homes they had in Zimbabwe, and one of the missionaries ended up selling it to me at market value, which was soon to shoot through the roof.

It took me a year to get over the bitterness of what this man had done to me. At the time, I trusted people and thought I could take them at their word—and the lesson learned was costly. This man, who was touching the entire world with the gospel, was living a double life, and it both shocked and saddened me.

But God is faithful to His Word, which promises that He will cause all things to work together for His good. In the midst of that disappointment, God continued to increase our efforts to reach out to the refugees, and our work became the basis for an organization we launched called Compassion Ministries. This relief and development organization is a non-profit company that the church established to meet the needs of people—spirit, soul, and body—by ministering food, clothing, shelter, safety, and self-respect.

Today Compassion Ministries is one of the hallmarks of Hear the Word Ministries, and Compassion's outreach has expanded to agricultural development, small business and micro financing, emergency relief, AIDS/HIV work, an AIDS orphan foster-care program, and much more. Compassion Ministries employs ten people full time, and involves countless volunteers from our church. Here are some of the outreaches of Compassion Ministries.

Street people

Zimbabwe's sky-high unemployment and inflation rates mean many people are living on the streets, often in large communities in various places in the cities. These are not shiftless or lazy people who are unwilling to work. There is simply no work for them in the midst of a devolving economy.

Reaching out to street people is very different from reaching out to refugees. Refugees are desperate and usually willing to accept whatever help we can provide. Street people, on the other hand, have a natural suspicion of strangers. They live in their own world, scavenging in other people's rubbish, and it is difficult for them to trust someone who offers help.

Compassion Ministries' outreach to street people began during the drought years when there was no surface water available in most parts of the country. People were forced to dig holes meters deep in order to reach potable water. We distributed water, started a weekly feeding program, and handed out clothing and blankets. We also meet their spiritual needs through a street peoples' church that we launched in 1990. The pastor once lived on the street himself, so when he preaches, he has real impact because he knows what street people go through.

Nearly 15 years ago when England's Queen Elizabeth came to Harare on an official visit, the government decided to "rid" the city of street people. It burned the shacks in which some of them were living and left the people stranded. We took responsibility for these people, leased a property, and tried to teach them trades. As a result, they lived a better lifestyle, but they had no responsibility for themselves—and they became totally dependent on us.

That was a wake-up call to us, and we realized that meeting immediate needs should be only one part of our outreach. Our goal should not be to create a system of dependency, but rather to reform the society that results in people living on the streets in the first place. This can be done through Kingdom principles based on trust, value for life, and having an attitude of faith for wealth. The "system" saw these people as squatters and takers, but we saw them as potentially productive members of society who could effectively generate wealth for themselves and for the Kingdom.

Having that vision changed our outreach so that instead of giving them hand-outs, we began to empower them to fulfill their God-given purpose. The government gave us 170 hectares of land (about 350 acres), and we launched our Mari-Mari project. Three hundred men and children from our church cleared the land, and we eventually resettled 38 destitute families with whom we had been working for seven years. We taught them how to farm using zero-tillage—that is, without plows or animals that can degrade the soil through over-plowing and over-grazing. They use very little tillage yet get a huge return on their crops. We also helped them drill boreholes, gave them pumps for irrigation, and arranged for micro-financing loans. We even partnered with H.J. Heinz Company USA through their local franchise holder, which donated tomato seedlings and promised to buy all their tomatoes.

The goal of the program was to bring people to self-sufficiency. Today the Mari-Mari program has become a successful model that we are duplicating all over the country. In total, we have resettled 150 people and helped them to become self-sufficient by teaching them agricultural methods, animal husbandry, and environmental skills.

Making Up the Difference

During the latter days of the drought, I came up with a project called Making Up the Difference to help fund some of our Compassion Ministries' outreaches. We placed more than 2,000 empty plastic milk jugs in retail shops throughout the country where people could donate their spare change, which we used to help get food and aid to the people. We organized a huge advertising campaign to promote the program, and the jugs filled up so fast that our volunteers could barely keep up with emptying them.

We eventually raised millions of Zimbabwean dollars—but at an enormous cost. I never would have dreamed that something so successful in helping others could attract so much controversy. The support from other churches was for the most part great (although some took offense at the program), and a number of churches sent volunteers to help collect the money. But some in the community attacked us mercilessly. The advertising program we chose caused quite a stir, to say the least. For instance, we showed a table of people dining on a sumptuous dinner, while a waif of a child stepped into the room and said, "You can make up the difference." Perhaps it was the fact that the diners were mostly white, while the child was black.

Whatever the cause, we came under a tremendous amount of fire from the press, which started labeling the program the "Buckstopper." If one of our volunteers was late in picking up the money, the store manager would complain to us (and to the press) that so much money sitting on the countertop was a high risk.

A local radio personality was particularly outspoken against us, and eventually started her own relief program to raise money for animals. She was livid and relentless in her on-air attacks against us. Her rationale, which she broadcast on her talk show, was that people can help themselves but animals cannot.

I made a case to the station that she was able to canvass for money using free airtime, while we had to pay for all our advertising spots on the station that allowed her to discredit us. They censored her to some extent, but it was not long before she resumed her campaign against us at full force.

Making Up the Difference ended in failure because there were too many opponents, many of whom felt it was more important to feed starving animals than starving people. As the pressure mounted and criticism began to arise even from within the church, I felt compelled to give up the project. This remains one of the most painful experiences of my life. It was the first time I felt God had told me to do something that I lacked the faith, character, or perseverance to carry out. It was part of the difficult learning experiences of what not to do. To this day, I wonder what would have happened to Making Up the Difference if we had simply stayed the course. It might still be funding some of the critical issues we face in Zimbabwe today.

AIDS/HIV

One of those issues, of course, is the devastating impact that AIDS has had on the country. Zimbabwe has the highest rate of HIV/AIDS infection in the world. Among the root causes of this devastation are a combination of government neglect, lack of healthcare resources, promiscuity, and social reluctance to face up to the drastic measures required to reverse the appalling numbers.

The impact on our families has been extensive. Nearly ten percent of Zimbabwe's population are children who have lost both parents to the pandemic—nearly one million children. We believe that the long-term solution for these AIDS orphans is not to institutionalize them, so we have designed a fostering program that helps place children in family situations. It costs about US$25 a month per child for food, clothing, and education that ensures a future for these children who, through no fault of their own, find themselves in a horrific situation.

We have built a state-of-the-art solar-heated orphanage that houses 38 children who are treated to quality care, full education, and regular medical check-ups. As with everything we do in the ministry, we built this orphanage to be the prototype for similar caring units we desire to build throughout the country

Hear the Word Ministries funds all aspects of Compassion Ministries, including salaries for approximately 20 full-time staff. We do have partner churches in other countries, but most of the money for our work is raised in Zimbabwe. My goal as a pastor is to give church members a vision that this can be done, and that they are the ones to do it.

Compassion Ministries will continue to be the focal point of our church outreach to the poor and destitute.

These programs are time consuming, expensive, and labor-intensive, so we are designing them to survive more than one generation. As with all our programs, our greatest challenge is to do something that will perpetuate itself into future generations.

Through the program, we are not only building dreams, but also building people who are becoming productive members of the Kingdom. Ultimately our desire is for Zimbabwe no longer to be a nation that receives missionaries but one that sends missionaries, and that we can truly be called a church that interfaces with all people of all nations.

CHAPTER 7

Building People...Building Dreams

I n all that we do, our goal is to "build people and build dreams." As the word of God impacts people's lives and they understand their purpose for living, dreams begin to form in their hearts—dreams that give them a higher purpose for living. Psalm 37:4 says, "Delight yourself in the Lord and He will give you the desires of your heart" (NIV). The dreams and visions that God puts into the hearts of His people are always for the good of society, and will have a positive effect on their family, friends, and church. Ephesians 2:10 says, "For we are his workmanship, created in Christ Jesus to do good works, which God prepared in advance for us to do" (NIV). People who will let God lead them will dream big dreams and do great things.

Here are the stories of three HTWC members whose dreams are impacting our city and nation. They represent many thousands of others who have taken Christ at His word to disciple the nations (see Matthew 28:18).

Blessed to be a Blessing
by Jeff Mzwimbi, chairman, Victory Business Forum

When I first walked into Hear the Word Church, I had

been self-employed for five months as a financial consultant, and times were tough. I had secured one deal to restructure the debt portfolio of a small manufacturing company, and the fee from that deal would be enough for two months expenses for my family, but would not cover school fees for my son who was attending school in the United Kingdom. I was already one term behind in his school fees, and if the fees for two terms were unpaid, he would not get his school report. We did not have enough to keep him in school, yet there was not enough to fly him home and enroll him in a local school, either.

I had a US$100 note in my wallet, which I did not want to part with until things really became tough. That time had come. I took the note and seeded it into God's work believing Him for a hundredfold harvest.

Three weeks later, I received a call from an employer I had left more than two years earlier. Apparently auditors had been through their books and discovered that at the time of my departure the company underpaid my terminal benefits by about £7000. At the time, that was US$10,000— a hundredfold harvest of the US$100 note I had seeded into God's work! They were calling to ask for my address so that they could send me the money. It was enough to settle my son's outstanding school fees, fly him back home, pay for his fees at a local school, and support my family for another three months. The first thing I did was to pay a tithe of that amount, and since then I have never missed a tithe.

A few months later I met Strive Masiyiwa, who asked me to help him raise money for his telecom company, which was involved in ongoing litigation. He needed to focus on the legal side of the matter and he wanted me to look after the finance side. Once that was off the ground, I knew I could focus on my desire to start up a financial services company. He did not think that the problem would take more than four months to resolve, but the four months became two years of walking a journey of faith. I learned to believe God for everything. I saw miracles as God met our needs in amazing ways. To this day, I still cannot explain how we survived.

At the Action 98 Conference, I pledged Z$200,000 towards HTWC's building fund, which I planned to pay by December 1998. I failed to meet that pledge by that date because I did not have the money, but I refused to be released from the vow and paid it during the next year.

God continued to prosper me, and at the Action 99 Conference, I signed my first Z$1 million check toward the cost of hosting the Conference. I was left with less than Z$50,000, but God kept blessing me. Since then, I have signed a few checks for Z$1 million and was able to meet my building-fund pledge several times over.

Today, five years later, my net worth has grown substantially. I have an even bigger vision and believe God will bring it to pass. I live a life of seeding and harvesting. My harvest today is from yesterday's seed, and tomorrow I am expecting a harvest of today's seed. One thing I know is that I have failed to out-give God, and I know what it means for God to "pour out so much blessing that you will not have room enough for it" (Malachi 3:10 NIV). I have seen it.

As I have sown seed into the good ground of Hear the Word Ministries, I have seen a return that is more than a hundredfold, not just for me but for many others. The more I give, the more I receive, and I know that the wealth that has come my way is so that I can be a vessel for giving, because a fraction of it can see me live comfortably for the rest of my life. Abraham was blessed so that he could be a blessing to the nations. I believe this will break the poverty spirit in our nation and release our people into their true destinies.

World-Class Standards for Healthcare
by Dr. Matthew Wazara, MBChB

As a medical doctor and member of HTWM, I have been greatly challenged by many of the teachings that are a foundation of the church. One of the most challenging for me as an African Christian is the assertion that world-class standards can be achieved anywhere in the world—including here in Africa. This is a standard of excellence that the church not only gives, but expects of its members, and it is an unusually high standard for a church and for Africa in general. Because of the history of colonization and the traditional culture of Africa, there is a tendency to believe that there is a limit to what standards an individual may attain while a resident in Africa, and that to exceed these one would have to emigrate to the developed world. This has not been allowed to be the case at HTWM, where we are challenged to live by faith, and to expect from God all those great things that are seen happening elsewhere, to believe that God wants to bless us with them, too.

When I first joined the church, I had just returned to Harare from working in a small hospital in an outlying agricultural settlement. I came back with my dream of building a small medical practice—one doctor, one nurse, a few patients a day, and a nice life for my family and me.

Pastor Tom invited me to be a coordinator for a hospital project that the church was considering. As he shared his vision, he said it was going to be the largest private hospital in the country, a specialist hospital built in partnership with one of the world's major medical institutions. It would attract clientele not only from Zimbabwe, but also from Zambia, Mozambique, Malawi, and Botswana.

Imagine my shock. I had been to Boston as a medical student, and to my mind there was no way that the standard of medicine I saw there could ever be brought to this country—yet here we were partnering with names that I had seen only in renowned medical journals. Pastor Tom made a bold move and said, "If we are going to have a partner for our medical center in Zimbabwe, then we would like the best there is in the world."

That began to speak to my heart—that I should expect excellence and strive for it as well. As Pastor Tom talked to me about helping to build the dream, he was also building me. The church's vision changed and enlarged my own vision. As I started to organize doctors' meetings and interviews for the program, I began to see a much bigger picture. God's call was not just to give me a few patients a day. I could see how I could be a part of impacting an entire nation by serving that vision and helping to get it established. I have always had a passion for heart surgery because it is so desperately needed in Zimbabwe. At any give moment, 400 children need heart surgery in this country, and many of them die while waiting for an operation locally or for funds to be treated abroad. Suddenly I saw how my passion could become reality. The hospital we wanted to build would do five heart surgeries a week, and so in two years we would clear the backlog.

That changed my mind. I no longer wanted to be an employee, but an employer—a mover and shaker, a person of influence. I have never been the same.

While working on the plans for this medical facility, I also started a business with some friends that combined emergency roadside service and emergency medical care. It was through this experience that I was exposed to the biblical principles of conducting business. What a journey that was! God gave me the belief that I could grow this business around the country and it could actually become a nationwide company.

As the country's politics and economy declined, my business was greatly affected, and my main customer reneged on a contract. That has been the greatest journey in my walk of faith, but Pastor Tom walked with me and taught me the invaluable principle that adversity does not call for the man of God to quit but to summon greater confidence and faith. I held on, and I have walked a difficult three years. At times there has been no income—and my wife and I have four children. But Pastor Tom has taught me that our jobs are just one of the sources of blessing that the Lord has for us. If God has commissioned us, He will pay the bills. God has taken care of everything and I have had more favor and influence in my "desert experience" than any stage I can recall in my life.

I was looking for a church that would do something for me—feed me and make me strong. But Pastor Tom said, "You've come to the wrong church. I want you to identify what you can do for this ministry. You serve, and you be the doctor who will bring reformation to the health care in this country—and you'll see what God will do."

I am not waiting for any further instruction! It will take another two years for the full medical facility to be in operation, but I am not waiting for that to happen. We are starting satellite clinics to feed into that facility—now. That way when the full facility is established, it will find these clinics waiting for it. Each satellite clinic will be able to admit 30 patients, and will have family practice, an emergency room, a dispensary, pharmacy, x-ray unit, and mother and child clinic.

In each clinic, we will practice what we have been taught: We can provide the best medical care right here in Zimbabwe, and we can do it with excellence.

Freed From Rejection
by Mwaitireni Jessica Chapfiwa,
Xtreme Kids team leader (HTWC children's ministry)

Being born out of wedlock, I grew up with a spirit of rejection and suffered with an inferiority complex. It drove me to work very hard to earn a living to prove to my earthly father who had rejected me that I could live a decent life without his support, and could take care of my mother and my stepsisters. I worked with the Ministry of Foreign Affairs, and even served overseas representing the Zimbabwe government in foreign countries. It was a life of struggling to prove to everyone that I could do it, yet at home I suffered abusive language such as, "You will never amount to anything just like your mother." I also suffered rejection from a serious relationship with a man whom I truly believed would become my husband. I was a nominal Christian, but my understanding of my purpose in life became so distorted that I drifted aimlessly for a number of years. Through God's grace, I rededicated my life to Christ and have never looked back.

Even though I was privileged to grow up in a Christian family, I lived in a rural community that gave preference to boys over girls, so I grew up thinking my place was behind the scenes, not to be seen or heard. When I came to Hear the Word Ministries, that was my thinking. I had such low self-esteem, although no one would imagine it because I used to put up a face of cover-up. Through many of Pastor Tom's sermons at church and through lectures at the Bible School, which I attended for four years, I learned to discover my purpose in life. One lecture that Pastor Tom gave at Bible School particularly impacted me. It was called "Breaking the Bonds of Iniquity," and it helped me to reflect on my own bonds of iniquity. The Holy Spirit showed me areas where I needed deliverance, beginning with the low self-esteem that I had due to the spirit of rejection. I went through personal deliverance spiritually, not only through that teaching but many others that Pastor Tom and Pastor Bonnie taught at Bible School, Ladies Fellowship, and Church, and also through guests from abroad such as Dr. John Stanko who made me realize my true purpose in life.

One day as Pastor Tom was teaching on leadership at Bible School, he quoted from Isaiah 6:8. "Then I heard the voice of the Lord saying, 'Whom shall I send? And who will go for us?' And I said, 'Here am I. Send me!'" (NIV).

Then Pastor Tom asked us, "Who feels called by the Lord?" I was among those who raised their hands. The Holy Spirit had delivered me from a spirit of rejection, and I was now ready to "go" for the Lord.

A number of years ago when I was in Malaysia working at the Zimbabwe High Commission, someone spoke a prophetic word to me from Proverbs 22:6, "Train a child in the way he should go, and when he is old he will not turn from it" (NIV). At the time, I did not realize the significance of it, although my dream as a teenager was to become a children's doctor or nurse. Today I know that my purpose in life is not being behind the scenes, as I once thought, but rather to bring the good news of the gospel of Christ to young children—in this nation and beyond the borders. God has brought many opportunities for me to express my purpose. As I identified my passion for reaching children, I found I was not fulfilled at my secular job, and I applied for an early retirement from the government.

As I have pursued my dream, I have graduated with a degree in Biblical Studies from Hear the Word Bible School, a certificate in Hear the Word Leadership Equipping Track, and a diploma in child evangelism from Child Evangelism Fellowship Europe (Switzerland). Today I am involved with

Xtreme Kids, HTWM's children's ministry, where I personally reach 450 children every week in church, visit five or-
phanages with 250 children, and teach in three Good News
Clubs with 100 children, one of which is in Chikurubi
Prison. Imagine 800 children weekly! I am also writing man-
uals for Children's Ministry Leadership Training with Pastor
Alan Graham, who heads Xtreme Kids.

What would have happened if I had disobeyed the call?
Many of these children would not have heard the word of
God. In Xtreme Kids, we say, "The people who know their
God shall be strong and do great things"(Daniel 11:32 TLB).
I have gone from being a behind-the-scenes person, to discovering my purpose and passion in life, to pursing it. God
has surrounded me with people who have added value to my
life and helped me to get out of the "box mentality" into
which culture and heredity had put me. In turn, that makes
me want to make a difference in the lives of other people as
well, particularly children. My passion is "that they may set
their hope in God, and not forget the works of God, but
keep His commandments" (Psalm 78:7 NAS). "Building
people...building dreams" has become a reality for me, because as this church has helped to build and rebuild me,
they have also helped to build my dream.

CHAPTER 8

A Church for All Nations

If you are a pastor or in ministry, you may be wondering how on earth we accomplish all that we are accomplishing, even with a church of more than 4,000 members. "I can't even get people to tithe," you might say. Many churches cannot get past the 20/80 rule, which says that 20 percent of the people do 80 percent of the work. We do not have all the answers at Hear the Word Ministries, but I can tell you what has worked for us. As we "build people and build dreams," there are seven principles that we emphasize.

Principle one: We have tried to instill in our church members the important fact that the church belongs to Jesus, and we allow Him to build it the way He chooses. For many years, man has tried to build the church using his own traditional patterns and methods, but it is Jesus, not man, who is to build the church—both local churches and the universal Church. If Jesus is to do that, it is crucial that we lay aside our own preconceived ideas and traditions about church governance and allow Him to reveal His plan to us through His Word. He said, "I will build my church, and the gates of Hades will not overcome it" (Matthew 16:18b NIV).

Principle two: We emphasize the kingdom of God, and the expression of that Kingdom in the earth is the local church. According to the rules of the kingdom of God, we must work with other churches. According to the rules of the kingdom of God, we can minister in our businesses, in our schools, neighborhoods, and wherever we find ourselves. As citizens of God's Kingdom, our influence is felt but it is not structured. We teach people that once they begin to grow in their individual lives and are firmly planted and established in a local church, then they can become effective in establishing God's Kingdom. Every member of the body of Christ is responsible for the preaching and establishing of God's Kingdom in whatever sphere God allows them to work. "The kingdom of God does not come with observation," (Luke 17:20 NKJ), but comes in the hearts of men.

Principle three: We constantly keep our vision in front of our members because Scripture says, "Without a vision, the people perish." Our mission statement is, "To build a strong Word-based church in the city of Harare, meeting people's needs, spirit, soul, and body, and from there to impact the five nations of central Africa with the gospel of Jesus Christ." God's pattern for establishing churches is very clear in Scripture, particularly in the book of Acts. Acts 1:8 contains the commission given to the early church and is the mandate that we are supposed to carry out as a part of our genetic code: "You will receive power when the Holy Spirit comes on you; and you will be my witnesses in Jerusalem, and in all Judea and Samaria, and to the ends of the earth" (NIV).

Throughout the book of Acts, this pattern appears over and over again. A "beachhead" was established in a region in order for the church to advance throughout that region.

The church that was based in Jerusalem was able to spread the gospel into Judea and Samaria (see Acts 6:7). The church in Antioch spread it in Asia (see Acts 12:24). The church Ephesus took care of Europe (see Acts 19:20). This did not happen overnight. The first 11 chapters of the book of Acts cover a span of 10-15 years, yet the early church maintained a clear vision of their mandate. They were to establish beachheads, and from there advance the church throughout their appointed region.

Hear the Word in Harare has taken nearly 20 years to establish itself as a presence in the community, but during this time we have constantly kept our goal and vision in front of our members. We have begun outreaches into the region where God has given us our "beachheads"; in Mozambique, for example, God has given us great success in following the biblical pattern for growth. A former member of our church has even started a church in Ukraine that has more than 6,000 members. In the coming years, I believe God is going to greatly accelerate the pace of that expansion as we focus on carrying out the vision He originally sparked in my heart in 1982.

Only as we see the invisible can we attempt the impossible.

Principle four: As much as we believe in the church as the vehicle through which the family of God is established, God uses people as His instruments to do this. God's people establish churches and provide headship over them. Without this understanding, we will fail to be effective in establishing a church-planting ministry in the areas where God is calling us to go. Such people must be full of faith and the Holy Spirit (see Acts 6:5), and they must have a vision and a dream because only as we see the invisible can we attempt the impossible. They must be willing to risk, and they must persevere. As Winston Churchill said, "Never, never, never, give up." And as Lester Sumrall once told me, "Perseverance always outlasts persecution."

Principle five: We teach people that their Christian walk will deepen only after "identification, involvement, and investment." We help them (1) identify with the vision and leadership of the church; (2) get involved in the church through commitment, fellowship, and serving in an area of ministry in which God has gifted them, and (3) invest their time and resources. As they find a meaningful place of service where they are both fruitful and fulfilled, the result will be increase in their personal growth.

We also teach people that there is a difference between being a church member and a church partner. When they attend or even join the church, they can consider themselves members. Once they decide this is where God has planted them, however, we ask them to be willing to shoulder a part of the responsibility of developing the local church through commitment and involvement. That way they can consider themselves not just a member of the church, but a partner in the work of the ministry. We've created more than 25 different areas of ministry where partners can get involved and serve in the church, such as leading a cell group, ushering, sound, nursery, the worship team, and many other opportunities.

Principle six: We emphasize living a life of faith, trusting in a God who is faithful, and expecting Him to be exactly who is says He is. God reveals His character to us through His names, which we find throughout the Bible.

God is, for example, our Father. Scripture tells us that there is "one God and Father of all, who is over all and through all and in all" (Ephesians 4:6 NIV). If He is above, through, and in all, then fatherhood is the pre-eminent character of God, and we can trust Him as the perfect Father. He is also our provider, and like every father, has an innate quality to want to provide for His children. He revealed Himself to Abraham as Jehovah Jireh, the "God who provides" (see Genesis 22:14). Once we learn that, no obstacle great or small will seem insurmountable to us.

God is our healer, and reveals Himself through His name, *Jehovah Rapha*. He desires us to come into the knowledge of His healing power—mental, emotional, and physical. He is also our victory, revealing Himself as our banner of victory, victorious in every situation. He never wants His children to be anywhere but in the place of victory.

God is our shepherd, guiding us (see Psalm 23) and lighting a path under our feet (see Psalm 119:105). Although He requires us to lead and take responsibility for many situations, we do so with the constant understanding and knowledge that He is leading us. In fact, one of the greatest indicators of our maturity as believers is when we are led by the Spirit (see Romans 8:14).

God is also our protector. Hundreds of Scriptures, such as Psalm 91 and Psalm 23, exhort us to expect His divine protection in our lives. He will constantly draw us into places where we can learn to trust Him and lean on Him. Finally, God is ever-present, always with us—*Jehovah Shammah*. One of the greatest attributes of a believer is to see God in every facet of life no matter how good or bad the circumstances. If we truly believe this aspect of His character, when difficult times come we no longer look for the devil's involvement, but instead look for God's hand in the situation. It does not mean that God is responsible for every situation, but that we can see Him working in and through every situation, and can declare, "In all things God works for the good of those who love him, who have been called according to his purpose" (Romans 8:28 NIV). Dr. A.R. Bernard says that a good translation of that verse is, "Whatever happens in life is either sent by God or is used by God."

Principle seven: Cell groups are a lifestyle. That is one of our key elements in building Hear the Word Church. In order for our members to be effectively pastored and to be significant members of the church, they need to be in a cell group. In Acts chapter 2, no matter how large the church grew, every day the believers "continued to meet together in the temple courts. They broke bread in their homes and ate together with glad and sincere hearts, praising God and enjoying the favor of all the people. And the Lord added to their number daily those who were being saved" (vv. 46-47 NIV). In a church as large as ours, only through interaction in cell groups can we develop relationships and effectively make disciples. We tell people that to grow bigger (that is, to grow in influence as a community), we must become smaller (cell groups).

We feel so strongly about the importance of cell groups that we did without a building for 20 years. We rented facilities as we needed them so that we did not depend on a building but rather on the vibrancy of relationships. We started our first home cell meetings in 1984, and today we have 200 cells that meet all over the city.

By the early 1990s, our church had grown so much and expanded into so many outreaches needing facilities, offices, meeting space, and storage space that we knew the time had come for our own facilities. Our cell groups were firmly in place, and we knew with the right continued emphasis we could keep the focus on the cells being the church, rather than any building we might construct.

The story of how we built our church, which we call the Celebration Center, is full of miracles. From the beginning we wanted it to be a "center for reformation for the nations"—a community center that would serve as a platform for reaching not only the city, but also the rest of Zimbabwe and the neighboring countries with the gospel of Jesus Christ. We had no idea how God was going to do it, but we had already seen enough miracles to know that another one would not be difficult for Him.

Early in 1990, I was driving past a piece of land on the Borrowdale Road in Harare when I felt God say that is where we were to build our building. The only problem was that the land was designated as a "green belt"—meaning no development. We gathered all the information we could and went to the City Council to ask for the piece of land, but they turned down our request.

I began to look at other pieces of property and other buildings, but over the next five years continued to pray about the piece of property on the Borrowdale Road. Every year I would gather a delegation and we would make a pilgrimage to the city offices, much to the chagrin of the city planners. Every year they would tell us the same thing. Finally, after four tries, the man in charge told me never to come back again, and that even if land were being developed, it would not be available for a church.

I did not let that stop us, however. In the fifth year I returned once again to ask for the land, and to my surprise the man who was in charge had been replaced by his second in command. When he saw me enter the room, he said, "I've been waiting for you to come! We have 11.4 hectares [28 acres] of land for the Hear the Word Ministries Community Center."

It was the exact same piece of land that the Lord had promised me five years earlier, and the same land that I was told a year before would never be available for a church. That was the first of many miracles—and we would need many before the process was over. Within a month we had finalized details for the sales contract and the purchase price was set at Z$2 million. The only problem now was finding the money. At that time even ten percent of that figure—the amount needed for a down payment—was an overwhelming sum. We had saved Z$58,000, but we had nowhere to go for the difference. I presented the need to our congregation, we took up a special offering, and raised exactly enough for the down payment on the land.

It took two years to get the special consent needed to use the land as a community center with all the ancillary uses we wanted to secure. At the end of two years, we were required to pay the remaining Z$1.8 million to own the land and begin to build. Once again we challenged the congregation to help raise the money.

That was the first time I had ever received a single gift of Z$1 million. A woman in the church who had received a large settlement from a divorce sent an anonymous check to be opened on the Sunday before we were supposed to pay for the land. Needless to say, the joy of receiving the money spilled over into the congregation, and it also opened generous hearts to give the additional Z$800,000 to purchase the land.

One of the leading contractors in the city came forward with the best offer to build and was ready to begin work even with the onset of the rainy season. In November 1997, the equipment moved on site, and started work on the Z$19 million structure. For months it looked as if nothing was happening to the visible eye, but tons of cement were being poured into the ground for the foundations needed to hold up the superstructure. As we built, the rains kept filling the holes, and we soon found that the water table was only a couple of inches below the surface of the soil. Eventually, like fingers on a skeleton, the cement columns began to reach to the sky, and once again we were faced with the dilemma of how to pay for it all.

A trickle of money was coming in, but only enough to pay the interest on the work already completed. The deadline was now in place for the first major payment to the contractor, and we had no money. We hosted our annual Action Conference in May 1998, and our guest speaker was Wayne Myers, a missionary to Mexico and father of David who was responsible for my coming to Africa 19 years earlier. Wayne's theme all week was "living to give and giving to live." On the Sunday night after most of our guests had gone home, Wayne took an offering and a pledge from our congregation of approximately 2,000 members. A total of Z$15 million was pledged, which at the time was in excess of US$1.3 million.

Although this was an all-time record gift, it left us far short of the Z$19 million we needed to complete the super structure. The architect and our project manager somehow convinced the contractors to loan us Z$7 million and pay the interest only on the portion that we would use. This allowed us to begin to build a shell inside the super structure. It was not long before that was complete, and the roof was on. That meant another Z$7 million was due—and we had run out of money. Although the church members had been diligent in giving, we needed a miracle.

We had long ago resolved that we would not borrow money to build the building, but would rely on faith and pay cash. (As interest rates climbed to 72 percent, we were glad we made that decision!) Nor would we seek the help we needed from outside Zimbabwe. We believed (and still do) that the work of God in Africa can be financed within Africa, and that we can become a sending nation for the gospel of Jesus Christ.

Three days before the money was due, we were told that if we did not come up with the money, we would have to shut down the site. And that is when we got our next miracle. One of our members gave an enormous gift of Z$13 million, which at the time was equivalent to US$1 million. It was a staggering gift and allowed us to pay our debt and continue our building.

This money combined with the consistent giving of our church members allowed us to move steadily ahead. However inflation began to skyrocket in Zimbabwe, and the building that originally was to cost approximately Z$30 million suddenly had a price tag of more than Z$75 million and climbing.

No matter how hard we tried, it seemed as if we were never going to catch up with inflation, but God was calling us to greater levels of faith. We knew He wanted us to make the decision to continue to build with no apparent funding available, even in the face of runaway inflation. Every time we would trust God for the next phase of the building, somehow the money would miraculously appear through the faithful giving of our congregation from the smallest widow's mite to our businessmen and women. Many of these people had started their own companies, which seemed to grow right along with the vision of the church. As the need arose in church, their companies would experience unprecedented blessing, and they generously gave to the building fund. Many of them felt that God had called them into business to fund the gospel and the vision of Hear the Word Church. They all saw the building as the center from which we could accomplish our dream to reach the five nations of central Africa.

Time after time, we would come to critical deadlines, and God always provided the money—in spite of unbelievable inflation. At one point, the Zimbabwe dollar had slipped to more than 40-1 against the U.S. dollar, which raised the price of our building to well over Z$200 million. It seemed as if things were getting out of control, but God knew how to touch the heart of His people, and in our darkest hour one of our leading businessmen gave a gift of Z$86 million—US$2 million. With this injection of capital and the faithful giving of our congregation, we were able to take the building nearly to the point of completion.

But by May 2000, once again we faced the dilemma of not having enough funds to complete the building. By this time, the dollar was set at 57-1, and inflation was running nearly 120-1 (and climbing daily). God is not hindered by inflation or exchange rates, however, and He so blessed and prospered one of our businessmen—even in the face of the fastest-shrinking economy in the world—that he was able to give Z$120 million, or US$2 million.

As far as I know, these kinds of gifts are unprecedented in Africa. They speak of the great faith and zeal of the people of Africa for the God-given vision of our church. Needless to say, I was overwhelmed by the gift, and we were able to continue to bring the building to near completion.

All that remained was the purchase of chairs, which we had chosen to import from overseas (so that we could have a world-class standard in Africa) and the sound system. With inflation, these and the finishing touches would cost Z$360 million, which by this time was nearly US$1 million—but by now our faith had grown. We had seen God faithfully provide for five years. It was no longer a question of, "Would He provide?" but "How would He make this provision?" Once again God moved upon the heart of a businessman, someone whose business was not his own but dedicated to the kingdom of God.

As he gave the money, he said, "This is our building and we are in this together—and this is only the beginning." With faith like that, it makes me, as a pastor, look good. But the true heroes are the men and women who have faithfully given, year after year. Although we have had massive individual gifts, without the consistent giving of every member of the congregation, this building would not have been possible. They, along with our pastoral team and building committee, have remained true to the vision. At times when all of our resources were available, it seemed as though nothing was impossible to the church. Truly we have left an example for others to follow.

If your dreams don't scare you, you are dreaming too small.

Never before have the words of Scripture become so illuminated as they almost seemed to jump off the page in our day-to-day experience, particularly the story of Nehemiah who rebuilt the walls of the city of Jerusalem. Although we were surrounded by miracles during our building program, it was not without casualties along the way. It grieved me that some people left the church because of the building. Critics declared that we had gone mad and were building something extravagant and ostentatious, when in fact our intention was to build for future generations—and provide a launching pad for programs and ministries to meet the needs of people, spirit, soul, and body.

With the Celebration Center, our intention is not only to

have a home for our church, but to use the facility to do what the church has always been called to do: bring reformation to the society around it by using Kingdom principles. We believe it is immoral to build a facility that is used only one day a week and sits empty the other six days, so this Center is to be a multifaceted, multifunctional building that serves the community every day of the week. Many of the facilities within the Celebration Center are available to the community for cultural and community events.

Within the 100,000-square foot facility are a 3,700-seat auditorium, a 2,500-seat outdoor amphitheatre, state-of-the-art conference facilities, and facilities for all our children's ministries including a day-care center, nursery, and children's church for 1,000. The building serves as home for our Bible college, Hear the Word Ministries Training Center. There is even a cafeteria and coffee shop, both open to the public. However, we have already outgrown our office facility, and all our outreach programs including Compassion Ministries, the Mari-Mari resettlement and development program, and our relief and development work have to be administrated from rented office and warehouse space.

Our focus for the Celebration Center is the same as for everything else we do: "To build a strong Word-based church in the city of Harare, meeting people's needs, spirit, soul, and body, and from there to impact the five nations of central Africa with the gospel of Jesus Christ." The more we can interface with society, the more opportunity we have to genuinely meet these needs. So in addition to the home of Hear the Word Church and Hear the Word Ministries, this facility is a center for arts and cultural events, where community groups can perform and where we can share the creativity that comes with the Kingdom. It is a center for education where professionals and business people can receive sound teaching on business, government, family, and education—all with a biblical worldview. The recreation center gives families a place to recreate and fellowship in a wholesome environment. And the world-class conference facilities allow us to host not only our own annual Action Conferences, but also symposiums and conventions that will benefit the economy and educate members of the Zimbabwean community in the professions they represent.

CHAPTER 9

Vision: The Power Within You

I do not believe that things happen by accident in the kingdom of God. When I look at my congregation on Sunday morning, I see young men, young mothers, older men, pastors, missionaries, doctors, teachers, and business owners. What I see are seeds. Everything God does, He does with seeds. Seeds can either germinate and become something fruitful, or they can lie dormant—in some cases for hundreds of years. Unless a seed is put into the right environment, it can lay dormant forever.

All of us have tremendous gifts and tremendous power, which God has inherently put on the inside of us. It is God who brings people together—people with potential—but God Himself cannot release that potential. The law of seedtime and harvest is just that—a law. God said, "As long as the earth endures, seedtime and harvest...will never cease" (Genesis 8:22 NIV). We can have a church full of seed, but unless we do something with it—unless we become strategic and intentional about planting that seed—we will just have nice little fellowships and churches. God is calling His church to be more than that, and it begins with the seed. More precisely, it begins with the element that God always puts inside the seed, or inside our hearts, something that makes human beings unique from any other creature that God created. That element is vision.

Paul, a man of vision, said, "Now to him who is able to do immeasurably more than all we ask or imagine, according to his power that is at work within us, to him be glory in the church and in Christ Jesus throughout all generations, for ever and ever! Amen" (Ephesians 3:20-21 NIV, *emphasis added*). The King James Version puts it this way: "Now to him who is able to do exceedingly, abundantly, above all that we ask or think, according to the power that works in us."

Big dreams need a big God.

This scripture astonishes me because, frankly, I have a pretty big imagination. He can do more than I can imagine? He can do more than I can think? And He says, "I'm going to do this according to the power that works on the inside of you." What is that power? Most people will say it is the Holy Spirit. I believe the Holy Spirit has a lot to do with it, but that is not the power that works on the inside of us, because everybody gets filled with the Holy Spirit, but not everybody does much with what they get filled with.

So what is this power? I believe it has something to do with asking and imagining. What makes human beings different from any other creature on the planet? It is the ability to dream, to have vision, and to see something. If you can see it, you can do it. God intended for you to dream, to have a vision and then bring that vision to pass.

Everything God does is according to a pattern based on a principle. If we can find the pattern and live by the principle, we can get the result that God designed. I spend my life looking for patterns and principles, then doing all I can to apply those patterns and principles. One of God's patterns and principles is that power always creates form.

In Africa, our rainy season starts in the middle of November. When you are trying to lay a parking lot for a new building, you do not need rain, because when it rains in Africa, it comes down like a Texas gully washer. It rains and rains, and the power of the rain pounds the earth, and as all that water starts to build up, it moves on the earth and it cuts new rivers and streams right into the earth, forming giant river valleys. The power creates the form.

God tells us in His Word that He hates churches that have form but deny the power thereof (see 2 Timothy 3:5). He said of the church in Sardis, "You have a reputation of being alive, but you are dead" (Revelation 3:1 NIV); that is form without power. As human beings, we like things that have form, even if they do not have power, because we are comfortable with the form—but God wants to see the power go forth.

God created you to be a carrier of vision, so that you can become powerful. Your vision will determine what you do in life. Now, you can take a short cut and corrupt your vision by trying to get something illegitimately or prematurely. And God will often let you try to do that, but the results will not be what God intended.

Nearly a quarter of a century ago, God gave me a vision for something that Bonnie and I are only now beginning to see happen. That is a long time to wait! But during the waiting time, we were true to that vision. We kept building on it and adjusting it as God gave us more information and clarity. It took patience and perseverance to carry the gift that God gave us. He told me long ago that He is interested in what we *become*, not what we *do*. God is not impressed by my building, nor is He impressed by my ministry title.

God is impressed by the character of a man—what we become in the process.

Psalm 37:4 says, "Delight yourself in the Lord and he will give you the desires of your heart" (NIV). People often think that this means that the Lord will give us what we desire, but that is not what the scripture says. It says He will actually put the desires into our hearts that He wants us to have. When it comes to catching a vision and a dream, we have to delight ourselves in the Lord—that is, put ourselves in a place where God can mold us and change us—and then He will give us the desires of our heart: dreams and visions worth living for.

We are living in an age where countries can no longer guarantee the safety of their citizens. September 11, 2001 changed all that. And, frankly, that is a good thing because although no government on earth that can provide blanket safety and security, there is a government that is being fashioned whose citizens will respond to a call when darkness covers the earth, the call from their God who says, "Arise, shine, for your light has come, and the glory of the Lord rises upon you" (Isaiah 60:1 NIV). There is a Kingdom that is beginning to emerge, and those of us who understand the Kingdom, and who take our dictates from the King of kings and the Lord of lords, are beginning to walk in a dimension that is not bound nor limited by the governments and kingdoms of this world. In order to do that, we have got to put ourselves under the rulership of the King of kings and the Lord of lords—and that means allow Him to put the desires, dreams, and visions into our hearts.

"The economy is doing really badly," you might protest. "How can I rely on dreams and visions?" The economy of the world doesn't have any bearing on Kingdom citizens. There is no economy worse than the economy in Zimbabwe; we have the fastest-shrinking economy in the world, yet in the midst of that there are Kingdom believers who are starting banks that will influence the banking industry in the entire country. There are Kingdom believers who will influence the telecommunications industry, who are bringing godly legislation before the political arena, who are bringing reformation to the medical and education arenas. This is happening not just in Zimbabwe, but also in the other nations of Africa as we begin to export a Kingdom-minded vision.

If we can do this in Zimbabwe, with the fastest-shrinking economy in the world, then you can do it anywhere else in the world. God is looking for someone into whom He can put His vision and power, someone through whom He can usher in the Kingdom—someone like you. God wants to give you dominion so that you take all those gifts and talents He has poured into you and use them for the Kingdom.

Here are eight principles concerning vision:

1) **Make sure your vision is from God.** How will you know you have accomplished what God has called you to do on earth if you have not seen the vision? God is not confused. He has a dream and a purpose for your life. God created you for good works. When you find out what God made you for and you do what God tells you to do, you can become the person you are supposed to be. When you are sure of your dream and your vision, it doesn't matter what everybody else is doing. I am amazed at how many people do not have vision from God, nor know their life's purposes. Find out why God created you and what God wants you to do, and then get focused and do it.

2) **Write the vision.** "Write the vision and make it plain on tablets, that he may run who reads it" (Habakkuk 2:2 NKJ). Write it down and make it plain, so that anybody who

reads it can "run" with it. If you have not written down your vision, then you do not have a vision; you are just playing games. Spend time on your vision, even if it means spending your whole life fine-tuning it.

3) **Expect God to intervene.** If your vision is so small that you can do it yourself, it is probably not a vision from God. You need to say, "God, if You don't show up, I won't pull through." Dream big dreams, and expect God to help you accomplish them. If you need answers from God on how to do that, do what Paul said and pray in the Spirit (see Romans 8:26).

Any vision that is worthy of heaven will suffer an attack from hell.

4) **Expect attack.** Any vision worthy of heaven will experience an attack from hell. Many Christians have never engaged the enemy; they have only engaged the conditions of their warfare. When a sergeant major orders a soldier into battle, the soldier does not reply, "I don't think I want to fight today because it's too wet or too cold, too hot, too cloudy." Those are just the conditions of warfare. The enemy is out there in the rain and snow, and he never lets up. It doesn't matter what the conditions are; he is out there. He is not worried about his comfort level during battle, and you cannot be either, or you will never do anything to stop him. You have to take your vision right out there on the battlefield, not be surprised when you come under attack, nor be slowed by the conditions you find on the field. If you have a vision, nothing can stop you, but if you are always worried about your comfort, you will never

get to your vision. It is not about you—but it is up to you. Your attitude determines everything.

5) **To obtain your vision, you will be stretched.** You will be put into situations where other people have failed, and where you will be tempted to give up. Sadly, other people (and perhaps other Christians) will be the ones encouraging you to stop. When God gives you a vision, there will always be people who will pull you down. The most difficult thing is to lovingly disconnect from your peers. I know because I experienced it firsthand early in my ministry. If you truly want to see the fulfillment of the vision that God gave you, you have to lovingly disconnect from those people. Stop playing with the turkeys and start flying with the eagles!

6) **Be passionate about your vision.** If I mentioned the name "James Dobson," you would think of Focus on the Family. If I said "Billy Graham," you would think of evangelism. If I were to say your name, what would people think of? People know you by your vision, by what you are passionate about, so get passionate about your dream and let other people hear about it. If you got your vision from God, it is worth sharing and worth giving your life for.

7) **Consult others who are successful and wise** (see Proverbs 15:12 and 22:17-18). Take a rich man to lunch! If you have a vision or a dream, find somebody who is already successful, take him or her to lunch, and spend the time asking questions. Find out all you can, successes as well as mistakes made along the way. That talk with an established person will get you places, and you might even find the key to success for your own vision. People who don't have a vision wait for something to fall into their lap, but if you have a vision, then go out and experiment, and trust God to help

you. Feed your vision and give it something to work with.

8) A person without a vision is a person without a future. A person without a future always returns to his past. That is why the police always ask suspects where they are staying and who their friends are; they get a full background so that the next time the person messes up, they know where to find him.

Martin Luther King, Jr., once said, "If a man is not willing to die for his beliefs, he is not worthy to live." Another man said it this way: "Some people live their lives so carefully so as to arrive at death's door safely." People should be able to die believing for something great, rather than to live, and die wondering if they could have done something great.

Someone once asked Helen Keller, "What could be worse than being born blind?" and she replied, "Living your life without vision." Vision transcends everything. Let the Dreamgiver fill your mind and heart with something big.

CHAPTER 10

Seasons of Purpose

In the previous chapter, I quoted Habakkuk 2:2 about writing down the visions that God has given you. The next verse says, "For the revelation awaits an appointed time; it speaks of the end and will not prove false. Though it linger, wait for it; it will certainly come and will not delay" (verse 3 NIV).

When God created man, His original intent was for us to rule, to reign, to govern, and to have dominion. That is the overarching purpose of man. Our purpose is the same, but the manifestation of that purpose is different for each individual. We don't all manifest our leadership the same way. We don't all have the same sphere of dominion or the same level of authority. Nor do each of us progress toward understanding or fulfilling our purpose at the same pace or schedule.

Right now the purpose of my life is to give oversight to Hear the Word Church and Ministries, to raise up and train future generations, and to advance the vision God put in my heart more than 20 years ago. That is my role. Someone else may be involved in that same purpose, but their role is different—perhaps to administrate that vision, or to hold us financially accountable for that vision—and therefore the timing and expression of their dominion and rulership is different from mine. The fulfillment of a purpose will go through seasons. The only thing that is "til death do us part" is marriage. Everything else is seasonal. You need to know the times and the seasons for your life. There was a time when I was anointed for evangelism, but I remember the day when I felt God turn off the burner of evangelism and turn on the burner of pastor. Later He turned off that burner, too, and I went through tremendous pain and agony disengaging from all the people I had pastored. My nature is to want to touch all the people and to know their names, but I sensed God saying, "You can grow to only about 200 people that way." He was calling me to another purpose, and I went through a painful process of disengagement to get there. Now I see the benefit, and I live my life vicariously through my spiritual sons and daughters—the ones whom I raised up and trained to pastor. Now it is their season to pastor.

No matter how painful the process, if you understand that God takes you through seasons of life, then when you move into the next one, you will be much happier and content. If you don't make these transitions, you will get stuck in a rut and never fulfill God's call on your life.

What you are doing right now may not be your final purpose, but you are laying the groundwork for its eventual fulfillment. God never wastes anything in your life. As I look back at my life and all I have done, good and bad, I realize that what I am doing now is built on everything I have ever done and learned in the past. Ecclesiastes 3:1 says, "To everything there is a season, a time for every purpose under heaven" (NKJ).

The time on a clock is chronological; it ticks away, and you cannot control it. This is *chronos* time, but there is another type of time called *kairos*, from the Greek word meaning "a fixed or definite period, a season." Kairos refers to a "season of time," and it is the type of time in which God operates. It has nothing to do with chronological time. God does not care how many years it takes to get you into a season; rather, He orchestrates your life so that you can become what He intended you to become from the beginning of time. Why? So that you can fulfill His purpose for your life.

You can be so worried about chronos time that you miss the kairos moment you are in—and thus miss the purpose of God for you in that season. Jesus' purpose was to destroy the works of the devil (see 1 John 3:8). Then why did He have to be born in a manger? Why did He have a normal upbringing? Why did not He just come to earth and have a showdown with the devil as the Son of God?

The answer is because of God's timing, and because God is a just God, even in His dealings with the devil. Genesis 3:15 states that God's divine intention was to get man back into right relationship with God. He said that the seed of Mary would crush the devil's head. He was talking about Jesus, but in the bigger picture He was talking about the church because you and I are in Christ, and are part of the body of Christ that is crushing the enemy.

There was timing involved in Jesus fulfilling His purpose on earth. He left you an example to follow in the Word. You can recognize what time or season you are in by studying the stages that Jesus went through to fulfill His own purpose.

1) **Time of initiation.** This first stage can also be termed the "call" or the "invitation to serve." Every one of us has a time of initiation. When God called me in 1972, He said, "You will be in Rhodesia." I had no idea where Rhodesia was, or even what it was, but God extended to me a call, an invitation to serve.

Luke chapter 2 gives another call. When Jesus' parents found Him after a frantic search, He replied, "'Why were you searching for me? Did not you know I had to be in my Father's house?' But they did not understand what he was saying to them" (vv. 49-50 NIV). This was the moment when the Father was initiating Jesus into ministry.

The word initiated means "to cause or facilitate the beginning of something; to begin to have knowledge of something." It is when you receive your invitation to serve. Until this point, Jesus had been just another compliant Jewish boy. If He was ever going to fulfill His purpose, however, the time had to come when He began to be above average. If He had remained under the control of His parents forever, He would never have accomplished His own purpose.

During times of preparation, God is not making you wait; He is making you ready.

When God begins to reveal His purpose in your life, you need to set apart time and energy to seek Him. Often there will be times when you will not be able to rely on the support of those closest to you. You have to hear from God on your own, and that may mean separating yourself from anything that hinders you from hearing. The hardest thing in life is to go to the next level, because it means initiating change and disengaging from where you are. God may want to initiate it, but you can get trapped in the old season. Change has to start somewhere, and usually God places a simple but deep desire in your heart. Your purpose begins when you start seeing a need, and you ask God, "How can I

fulfill it?" He says, "I want you to fill that need." Follow the
needs you see, and you will be amazed at how you will find
your purpose.

2) **Time of preparation.** In that same passage from Luke,
Jesus could have responded differently to His parents. He
could have said, "Look, I'm the Son of God, and I'm staying
in this temple. This is what I'm called to do." Instead He
went home with them. "Then he went down to Nazareth
with them and was obedient to them" (Luke 2:51 NIV). He
spent the next 18 years learning a trade that He would
never use because the Father was preparing Him for His
purpose: to destroy the works of the devil. He did not do
that the first day He arrived on earth. He was born in a
manger, served His mother and father, and worked in a carpentry shop. Until the day He was 30 years old, He did
nothing toward His purpose except to prepare for it.

Through the crafts of carpentry and fishing, Jesus
learned many things that would help him later in life and
ministry. What did King David do after Samuel anointed
Him as king? He went back to tending sheep for 15 years,
serving his father as a shepherd boy. God initiates, and He
follows it with a time of preparation. Just because you get a
call from God does not mean you abandon reality. This is
where so many people in the body of Christ miss God's
kairos timing. They receive the call, and they want to jump
into it with both feet—immediately. That did not work for
Jesus, so why should it work for you? You need to go
through the season of preparation. You will learn the same
thing that Jesus and David learned: faithfulness. Paul told
Timothy to find faithful men and entrust the gospel to them
(see 2 Timothy 2:2). God needs faithful men and women
who can endure the difficult times.

You must understand that God is not in a hurry no

matter how much you are. Just like the prodigal son, you can demand your inheritance before you are mature enough to handle it. During times of preparation, God is not making you wait; He is making you ready. Knowing your purpose does not automatically qualify you to fulfill it. "So do not throw away your confidence; it will be richly rewarded. You need to persevere so that when you have done the will of God, you will receive what he has promised. For in just a very little while, He who is coming will come and will not delay" (Hebrews 10:35-36 NIV).

3) **Time of inspiration.** This is when God begins to inspire you to serve, and when He empowers you to do so. When Jesus was baptized, the Father's response was, "You are my Son, whom I love; with you I am well pleased" (Luke 3:22 NIV). Until you are inspired to believe that you are "His," and that He is "well pleased" with you, you will never fulfill the purpose of your life.

It was not enough for Jesus just to initiate or prepare Himself. He needed the inspiration—the anointing and enabling power of the Holy Spirit—to fulfill His purpose, just as we do. It is the anointing of the Holy Spirit that breaks the yoke of bondage. Inspiration is a divine influence on a person to qualify Him to receive and communicate sacred revelation. Inspiration means "to influence, to guide or move by supernatural power, to draw forth or to bring out." It is the anointing without which you can do nothing. Jesus needed the enabling power of the Holy Spirit to fulfill His purpose; how much more do you need it to fulfill yours?

The anointing is what gives you the courage to be different, to dare to do the impossible. The anointing may require you to be outstanding, or different. When it gets on you, you will be required to do things that appear to be a bit foolish at times. So many people resist the Holy Spirit because they do not want to be different, but you must not turn down the gift of inspiration to do the unusual and the extraordinary. That is what your purpose may cause you to achieve. You need the anointing to fulfill your purpose and to see your visions come to pass.

4) **Time of temptation.** Jesus could not destroy an enemy He had never faced. It was imperative that He was able to look at the enemy square in the face and resist any form of compromise that he might offer. To tempt means "to entice to do wrong by promise of pleasure or gain." Temptation is to take the immediate gain over the long-term purpose of your life. James 1:13-14 shows that temptation never comes from God, but out of your own heart.

When the Spirit led Jesus into the wilderness, He did not lead the devil there to tempt Jesus. God will lead you into a place with Him, and there will come a time of temptation in your life. Anytime there is a gift or call, it will be tested, and temptation will come. The enemy wants you to get off course and miss your kairos season and timing because he knows if you ever get what God really has for you, you will have the power to affect the lives of so many people around you that you will be a threat to his kingdom. Many people say, "I would give everything..." That is indeed what it will cost you to get what God has for you: everything.

5) **Time of motivation.** God gives you a purpose in life, but in order for you to fulfill it, in most cases it requires the cooperation and assistance of other people. Jesus could not have accomplished His purpose on the earth without motivating 12 disciples to follow Him. Twelve men decided they would stick through it to see Him fulfill His purpose. No man is an island, and if your purpose is to be a Spirit-filled lawyer, doctor, or teacher, you need to motivate people

around you to support you and help you do what you were
born to do.

6) **Time of validation.** This is the season when you begin
to operate in the authority that God gave you. Matthew 4:23
says, "Jesus went throughout Galilee, teaching in their syna-
gogues, preaching the good news of the kingdom, and
healing every disease and sickness among the people"
(NIV). When Jesus began to walk in His purpose, the Father
validated His ministry with signs and wonders. Similarly,
when you begin to walk in your purpose, God will validate
your ministry. He will make it apparent to everyone that He
is with you, that He has called you and anointed you. The
Bible says that signs follow those that believe (see Mark
16:17).

If you are walking in your purpose, eventually it will be
apparent even to skeptics. You should not rely upon opin-
ions of course, but validation will come to those who are
anointed to serve.

7) **Time of separation.** When you commit to God's purpose, regardless of what it is, there will come a day of separation. The word means "to set apart, to become distinct, to
be secluded or solitary or individual." In one day, Jesus
went from the Last Supper with His disciples, to asking
three of the closest ones to pray with Him for an hour, to all
three falling asleep all three times that He asked them to
stay awake. Then He agonized over what He was facing, and
prayed to His father to remove the cup. His own Father did
not answer Him because drinking that cup was part of what
He was born to do. Later the same day, a man with whom
He had traveled for three-and-a-half years betrayed Him,
and another of His closest companions denied Him three
times, even as He was standing in the face of His accusers.
Finally, all 12 ran away.

When you are separated for a purpose, it says to God, "I will fulfill this, even if I have to stand alone." If you do say that, you must understand that the day will come when you will have to live it. There will come a time when you will feel isolated and will stand alone. God did not cause the disciples to sell out Jesus; it is the human nature of man that can fail you in your greatest hour of need.

All of us want validation, but many do not want the separation. Unless you are willing to leave father, mother, homes, and all the rest, you will never fulfill your purpose in life. It is the nature of humans to pat you on the back when all is going well, and to stab you in the back when you are in your darkest hour of need. What are you going to do when that happens—throw in the towel just when you are so close to actually fulfilling your purpose? Or are you willing to stand alone if necessary to see things through to the end?

Let us fix our eyes on Jesus, the author and perfecter of our faith, who for the joy set before him endured the cross, scorning its shame, and sat down at the right hand of the throne of God. Consider him who endured such opposition from sinful men, so that you will not grow weary and lose heart" (Hebrews 12:2-3 NIV).

If you are in a season of separation, you must hold tight, because the next season will make it all worthwhile.

8) **Time of manifestation.** This is the time you have waited for—the season when you actually see your purpose manifested in its fullness. After an agonizing season of separation, Jesus fulfilled His purpose: "And having disarmed the powers and authorities, he made a public spectacle of them, triumphing over them by the cross" (Colossians 2:15 NIV).

If Jesus had to go through these steps to find His purpose, how much more will you?

CHAPTER 11

The Challenge:
What About *Your* World?

Faith activated by hope done in love will produce a miracle—and what has happened is Zimbabwe is definitely a miracle. As we close this book, my question to you is this: If God can perform miracles in a country with severe drought, political turmoil, racial prejudices, off-the-charts inflation, the highest rate of HIV/AIDS infection in the world, and, the dubious honor of the fastest-shrinking economy on the planet, what can He do in your world?

What change do you long to see in your country? What part of your city does God need to touch? You cannot use poverty, difficult political situations, or racism as an excuse not to act because God is overcoming all of those in Zimbabwe, and He is using His church to do it. It is my belief that if the church in Zimbabwe not only can survive but can help build companies, invest in the future of the nation, and leave an inheritance for their children's children, then it is living proof that the blessing and prosperity of the kingdom of God can be experienced by anyone, anywhere in the world.

What challenges do you face? Can you believe that Jehovah Jireh, the "God who provides," will meet your needs, as He has met ours? What dreams and visions do you have? Perhaps you have dared to dream big dreams for God, only to see them pulled down before they got off the ground. Perhaps others have pulled them down; perhaps you have done it yourself. Consider these responses:

"Airplanes are toys of no military value."—*Ferdinand Foch, 1851-1929, French soldier and professor of military strategy*

"The mission Columbus has proposed is folly...The Atlantic Ocean is infinite and impossible to traverse."— *Talevera Commission, 1491*

"There is no need for the Patent Office. Everything that could be invented has been invented."—*Head of the U.S. Patent Office in the 1890s*

"Who wants to hear actors talk?"—*H. M. Warner, 1881-1958, regarding the possibility of "talkies" replacing silent movies*

"We have reached the limits of what is possible to achieve with computer technology."—*John von Neumann, 1903-57, in 1949*

"There is a world market for maybe five computers."— *Thomas Watson Jr., 1914-1993, founder of IBM*

Perhaps none of these people had going for them what you and I have going for us: Belief in a big God. Someone once said, "If your dreams don't scare you, your dreams are too small." Big dreams need a big God, and big problems need a big solution—and a big God to find that solution. Only as we see the invisible can we attempt the impossible.

Jeremiah cried out, "Oh, Sovereign Lord, you have made the heavens and the earth by your great power and outstretched arm. Nothing is too hard for you" (Jeremiah

32:17 NIV). When you face challenges and problems that seem overwhelming, it is only the bigness of God that will give you the solution to those problems—and the grace to persevere to the end. Unless you see the ultimate, you will be enslaved by the immediate.

From my years flying a plane, I know that pilots are often directed to a beacon so that they can get a bearing in order to find the runway. God does the same thing: He gets you to something you can see so that He can get you to something you cannot see.

God is concerned not only with your life in eternity, but also your life here on earth. He has a plan for you for eternity, and He also has a plan for you here on earth. Too many Christians think that life on earth is just a "waiting room" for heaven, but in reality God has a Kingdom lifestyle planned for each of His children in order to bring you to a place of purpose, prosperity, and significance in Christ. Accepting Jesus as your lord and savior should be the first step in discovering the will of God for your life here on earth—yet many Christians never get past the first step.

Reformation of nations will not take place at the barrel of a gun—although some will try. Nor will it necessarily take place at the ballot box—although that is a valid and cherished right. The cultural transformation that I believe God wants His people to effect in their cities and countries must begin with a change of heart in the individual. When we genuinely surrender our lives in their entirety to Christ, we no longer live for ourselves but for Him. One person's life has the power to transform a family; one family has the power to affect a church; one church has the power to affect a community; one community has the power to affect a city; one city has the power to affect a nation, and one transformed nation can affect an entire continent—or the world.

"Your kingdom come, your will be done on earth as it is

in heaven" (Matthew 6:10 NIV). This is my dream, and because of this dream I have spent my life building people and
building dreams. The prophet Daniel not only predicted this
great Kingdom, but he also said, "The people who know their
God shall be strong and do great things" (Daniel 11:32 TLB).
This is the hour to do great things for God.

Your consistency will take you further than your qualifications and your training

------

I came to Africa nearly a quarter century ago, in the
midst of a civil war, with no support, and no idea how to be
a missionary or a church leader. Bonnie came here not long
after that—a professional singer who never had any desire
to be a missionary or a pastor's wife. In spite of our limita-
tions and frailties, we have seen God fulfill every dream and
vision He put in our hearts. I always tell people, "Your con-
sistency will take you further than your qualifications and
your training."

It has not been without hardships, as Bonnie and I have
endured years that were as turbulent as the history of this
nation. We have survived droughts both natural and spiritual, but in every season the Lord has been abundantly
faithful to us. It has taken 20 years to see a dream begin.
Dick Mills once prophesied to me, "God's glory in the last
days will exceed His glory in the early days ten times over."
I believe that this is the beginning of a great outpouring that
will sweep across not only Zimbabwe, but all of central
Africa.

On the day we broke ground for our new Celebration

Center, God sent another encouraging prophetic word: "Do not look at the small things, but look at Me, for I'm a miracle-working God. As you start to look at Me, don't look at the small things but at the greatness of who I am and what I can do."

God working through you can result in miracles. A number of years ago, Bonnie wrote a song called The Answer, which was a response to difficult questions such as, "What is the answer to poverty? To AIDS? To injustice, hatred, and hunger?" Her song gave the reply:

> The answer is shelter.
> The answer is food.
> The answer is Jesus.
> The answer—is you.[11]

In the book of Acts, Luke describes a scenario that we could call the reformation of a society:

> *Philip went down to a city in Samaria and proclaimed the Christ there. When the crowds heard Philip and saw the miraculous signs he did, they all paid close attention to what he said. With shrieks, evil spirits came out of many, and many paralytics and cripples were healed. So there was great joy in that city* (Acts 8:4-9 NIV, *emphasis added*).

When the Word is preached in a city with signs and wonders following, the result is great joy in that city. It is God's will that we bring great joy to our cities and nations. God is looking for Philips who will do that. God is looking for you.

Endnotes

1. "Citizenship in a Republic," speech by Theodore Roosevelt at the Sorbonne, Paris, April 23, 1910.

2. Now that I am a pastor, I definitely do not recommend this pattern, and I counsel singles to do as I say and not as I did!

3. It took ten years before I was finally vindicated. Not long after this incident, the pastor who made the charges against us left the country and moved to New York, where he headed the CFN school there. Only ten years later, after he was accused of embezzling money and his own marriage failed, did Mrs. Lindsay finally understand the truth of what had happened. She realized she had accused me falsely, and offered to fly me to Dallas. There, this great woman of God graciously sought my forgiveness for something from which I had released her nearly nine years earlier. Mrs. Lindsay was gracious and humble, and she remains one of the truly great generals of the faith.

4. *The World Factbook.*

5. *Culture Matters*, edited by Lawrence E. Harrison and Samuel P. Huntington, © 2000 by Basic Books, page 48.

6. *Ibid.*

7. This is an African term for anyone of mixed racial heritage.

8. *The World Factbook* (2001 figures).

9. *Ibid.*

10. *Operation World,* by Patrick Johnstone and Jason Mandryk, © 1993, 1995, 2001, Paternoster Lifestyle

11. "The Answer," music and lyrics by Bonnie Deuschle, © 1991 by Bonnie Deuschle. Used with permission.

FOR MORE INFORMATION:

Hear the Word Ministries
Hear the Word Publishing

AFRICAN OFFICE:
162 Swan Road
PO Box HG 88
Highlands, Harare
Zimbabwe
263 (4) 850880
postmaster@htwm.co.zw

U.S. OFFICE:
PO Box 764707
Dallas, TX 75376
(469) 939-0833
(214) 566-2966
htwmus@aol.com